By

Pastors Michael and Judith Magel
Co-authored with Jeannie Hill

Preparing Yourself For Dr. Jesus To Lead You Into The Operation Of The Gifts of Healings

The Merry Magels
Mike & Judi

John 14:12

This book is a work of non-fiction.

ISBN:1533571295
ISBN-13: 978-1533571298

Special thank you to Rev. Jon O. Nessle for consultations

Cover Art
by Leah M. Baker
artbyleahmarie@gmail.com

Stock imagery by Shutterstock
Image 116958256, Image 49984714

ACKNOWLEDGMENTS

Special thanks to all those who allowed their testimonies of very private situations to be shared publicly, for the help and healing of others.

DEDICATION

This book is lovingly dedicated to our son, Eric, and his wife, Amy Magel, our daughter, Michelle, and her husband, David Nosker, as well as our five grandkids Branden, Mackenzie, Mallery, Ethan, and Ashleigh Nosker.

God Shots

PREFACE

The first thing we prayed for and healed was a dog.

We're just Mike and Judi Magel, nothing special about us. It is Dr. Jesus and The Holy Spirit who do all these wonderful things. We just pray for people and it is Dr. Jesus and the Father God who gets the Glory.

In this book, you will see scripture references we believe are the foundation for the results that we have seen and also, we relate stories or *testimonies* from the people who were healed. Testimonies defeat the devil ***(Romans 12:11)***, which we will discuss in detail and they also build encouragement, bring comfort and promote healing in others as they are told. All testimonies in the book have been authorized for use by the people mentioned in the testimony.

We will review in scriptures about healing which is in the physical category but it also includes deliverance ministering, or removing spirits that affect the physical, just as Jesus did. At least 23 references to this are in the gospel accounts of

Jesus' ministry on earth and we want people to understand this is just a part of a healing ministry.

We will answer the most frequently asked questions that we get when we are with people and we want to emphasize that we all, already have the ministry, the authority and the commission to "*heal the sick, cleanse the lepers* and that *these signs shall follow those that believe...they shall lay hands on the sick and they shall recover." **(Mark 16:17 & 18)***

Though we wanted to leave a record for our families, we want people to know the purpose of this book is not calling attention to ourselves, other than the fact that we are just people. Though we are both ordained ministers, we were not when we started our healing ministry with God.

"Every-day work" is the reason that we wanted to call attention to the fact that God will work with any person who wants to work with Him. As somebody once said, "*Just be humble enough to do the crazy things God tells you to do".*

We also reference other people who are currently,

or who have been healers and pioneers in healing ministries like Charles and Frances Hunter (deceased). We mention ministries; Christian Family Fellowship and Reverend Tonia Shroyer and Reverend Wayne Clapp, Rev. Kevin Guigou, Rev. Tom Dill, Christian Retreat and Pastor Phil Derstine in Sarasota, Florida, Dr. Roberts Liardon and Pastor Billy Burke, Prophet Ben Smith, all of whom we have studied under and we thank them for their lives of service and connections with us.

Final Note: by co-author and editor, Jeannie Hill:

I have tried to convey not only the historical documentations of healings and journeys of Mike and Judi Magel accurately as they described them to me, but also, in conveying it with the very special and particular nuances that make Mike and Judi the wonderful people that they are. I would only add that if you step out of the box of your own making called Your Life Right Now and ask *What Can God Really Do?,* you will be seeing more signs miracles and wonders!

Mike began by asking,

"So did I tell you about the dog?"

CONTENTS

1 Why "God Shots"?

For some time we have been encouraged by friends to write a book on healing. We have put it off mainly because we didn't want people to think we are special or unique.

Mike: I call Jesus, *Dr. Jesus,* because he is the healer. We never started out to do anything like we have done; we just did the things God told us to do in the name of Jesus, and that has kept us in a constant state of change in our retirement.

We like to say that we are *refired*, not retired. Judi and I have been married 54 years and things just keep getting sweeter. The things we have seen God do in front of our very eyes, well, people just kept asking us if we were going to write a book, so

we decided we would.
The only real special thing about us is that we have the Holy Spirit in us. *We have this treasure in earthen vessels, that the excellency of the power may be of God, and not of us.* ***II Corinthians 4:7***
The only special name we have is that of a Son of God and that we are full of power. Put the two together and we have what we call a "SOGWAP". Definition: Son of God With All Power! Ever since the day of Pentecost, God has wanted His kids to know the Power of God that lives in a born-again believer. That same power that raised Jesus from the dead is not only ours to know of it, but to experience it, and, not only at the time of Christ's Return, but, in our everyday lives.

> ***Ephesians 1:19 & 20***
> *And what is the exceeding greatness of his power to usward who believe, according to the working of his mighty power, which he wrought in Christ, when he raised him from the dead, and set him at his own right hand in the heavenly places.*

Every-day people tapping into God's power, every day, is what *God Shots* is all about. We will explain the simplicity of God's power to us and how simple it is to see Him go to work by our hands and the words of our own mouths.

Why the name ***God Shots***? When ministering healing to a person, sometimes there are immediate results and other times, there is a time lapse. When a person gets a shot of penicillin, it may take a few days for the results to appear. It is the same with ministering; sometimes it may take several days. A miracle is immediate, or, a healing may take time. All healings are a gift, ***(I Corinthians 12:9)*** but all healings are not miracles that occur immediately.

It may take time to work, but be assured and comforted, knowing that God is not asleep, He has not delayed your deliverance and, He is at work. ***God shots*** are for any one, any where, any time !

Judi: Wherever we go, to a store, to the airport, to a restaurant, there is always opportunity to say the five most powerful door-opening words, *May I pray for you?* Mike and I will talk to anyone, anywhere and it is our friendly open way that gets people involved.

After talking with people, occasionally, people do

say "No thanks" when we ask if they want to be prayed for or ministered to, but, we can still pray for them on our own time. Most of the time though, people will accept the offer to be blessed.

We were on vacation and I was going off a ship at Grand Turk Island to go jewelry shopping; Mike wasn't even going to leave the ship, but at the last minute, he changed his mind. A group of young people were headed back to their ship and when they saw Mike's Ohio State ball cap, they stopped to talk about football. There went my jewelry shopping!

We told the kids of our healing ministry and that we would pray for them. Well, they were like hungry baby birds! One young man was showing his hip scars, one youngster said he was supposed to have shoulder surgery. We prayed for all of them, led three of them into the new birth and then they were on their phones telling other kids about it right then, all because Mike had on that ball cap. I got off the ship hoping to get good deals on jewelry but we got the diamonds of Joe, and Nick and Brandon, instead.

Mike: There was a time when Judi and I didn't say

much about the healing that happened at our hands. When we say that, we want to give credit where credit is due. The healing and deliverance we proclaim in this book are all done by God, the Father, His son, Jesus Christ, and by the power of the Holy Spirit, but it often does take a person saying or touching someone else to get the job done, just like Jesus did.

In addition, we finally recognized in God's Word (The Bible) that speaking about deliverance brings more deliverance to the people listening, and, when the person who received healing and deliverance shares it, the healing is reinforced and builds faith or believing in others. When the 12 and then the 70 anointed disciples returned, they “rehearsed” it, told their experiences to others.

> ***Acts 14:27***
> *And when they were come, and had gathered the church together, they rehearsed all that God had done with them, and how he had opened the door of faith unto the Gentiles.*

The purpose of testimonies can be found in Revelation.

God Shots

Revelation 12:11

And they overcame him (satan, the devil) by the blood of the Lamb, and by the word of their testimony; and they loved not their lives unto death.

Real healing from God; true shots from God, can be in several different forms. We know healing is through reading and hearing the written Word of God, through specific teachings, through physical touch; a caring hand or caress or through song but think on the times you have had someone say just one sentence to you that you needed to hear at that moment.

Sometimes when we pray, we ask God for specifics, sometimes we simply ask Him to fix the situation and often-times, when we quit trying to tell God how to fix it, the answer will come.

God's ways are His and we have found that if we will just do what He tells us, we have results that we never imagined. We will receive the God Shot or we will be able to administer one that targets the specific need at that moment in time. Perhaps you have done this yourself, not knowing exactly why you were inspired to say something but when you did, but, it was needed.

Judi: Testimonies; when somebody hears about something, they know about someone who has the same situation they do and God healed them through the spoken word, then they know it is available for it to happen to them. "*Faith cometh by hearing and by hearing the Word of God,*" (***Romans 10:17)*** and then, the healing can happen.

There are testimonies listed on many websites and sometimes, people who have had similar conditions have found each other and become friends, because of it.

Mike: What people need to do once they have been delivered is to continually praise God and Jesus for their deliverance, tell other people and engage in helping minister to other people to get their healing or deliverance. Testimonies are so big in the lives of Christians.

People who have received deliverance then declare this as a "testimony of their testimony". Telling the success of their situation then becomes a testimony again.

God Shots

Excerpts from the healing of Lynn A.

One Sunday morning at the (annual teaching) Family Reunion (at the CFF Ministry Church), I asked the Magel's if they would minister healing to me. Thirty years ago, I didn't realize how badly I'd injured my left knee which then underwent extensive open knee surgery....Three years ago, my car was rear-ended, injuring my back, neck, right should and both knees.

They (the Magels) began by rebuking the trauma itself and the pain, and carried on from there, ministering healing to both my knees and right shoulder and much more...to my hips and to specific areas of my back and neck, straightening and strengthening my spine and vertebrae, strengthening my tendons, ligaments and replacing cartilage and calling for padding and lubrication in my knees and removal of any arthritis that may have developed. God told them things I had not mentioned nor even considered.

As I stretched out my right arm next to my left, I saw my arm extend on their command, to match the length of the left arm! When I sat on a bench and stuck out my legs, they were of equal length! We praised God and His Son for the healing made available to me.

The Magels told me the adversary would try to negate the healing with sudden or increasing pain, but I was to recognize that and continue to claim my healing and restoration...

I told them I longed to bring healing to others, as they did so they told me, "You've got God in Christ in you, just remember to ask people, '*May I pray for you?*'"

They asked the woman sitting next to me on that bench those same words and then allowed me to minister to her with them! They ministered many things as God revealed to them and I got to see that woman's leg extend at their command to match the length of her other one.

Since then, I have stopped taking my pain medication and I have been walking very differently with my new knees. I can go up and down steps and am limp-free! I know that any pain I still experience is just my body adjusting to my healed parts and also an indication that I should strengthen certain areas that had become weakened by the former pain and years of reduced activity. I praise God all day long, and am excited at the prospect of doing that all my days!

Mike and Judi: We are writing this book because many people have told us that "they want to do what we do," which is, operate the gifts of healing as we see recorded in Corinthians.

> ***I Corinthians 12:9***
> *To another faith by the same Spirit; to another the gifts of healing by the same spirit.*

The truth is, every born-again believer has the same ability to operate the gifts of healing through the power of the Holy Spirit and the spirit of Christ that lives inside themselves. God is not a respecter of persons; but He is a respecter of conditions. That condition is that you have to operate your faith which you receive when you are born-again. You have already been given the power and authority. Most believers are not aware of their authority or the power that is within them.

Judi and I are by no means big-time theologians, or researchers of The Word, or have a bunch of degrees. We're just common folks who believe what The Word says and what Jesus accomplished on the cross. We have taught God's Word for some 40 years and we've learned to trust and rely on our Lord Jesus.

When we started telling our testimonies, it opened the doors for us. Testimonies are so powerful; they give hope, encouragement and serve as a faith-builder. We are not bragging on ourselves, but on our loving heavenly Father and our Lord, Jesus Christ. The only way we can please God is by believing and that is a big key in seeing results.

> ***Hebrews 11:6***
> *But without faith it is impossible to please him: for he that cometh to God must believe that he is, and that he is a rewarder of them that diligently seek him.*

> ***John 14:12***
> *Verily, verily, I say unto you, He that believeth on me* (Jesus), *the works that I do shall he do also: and greater works than these shall he do; because I go unto my Father.*

> ***Mark 11:23***

For verily I say unto you, That whosoever shall say unto this mountain, Be thou removed, and be cast into the sea; and shall not doubt in his heart, but shall believe that those things which he saith shall come to pass; he shall have whatsoever he saith.

Mark 9:23
Jesus said unto him, If thou canst believe, all things are possible to him that believeth.

Either Jesus told the truth, or, he lied. We choose that he spoke the truth. There is no time limit on this promise. It is to *whosoever*, now! This very time and hour!

Ephesians 1:19
And what is the exceeding greatness of his power to usward who believe, according to the working of his mighty power.

We have two children and five grandchildren, and hopefully, we will have great-grandchildren. We want them not to be ignorant of this manifestation of healing. The gifts of healing can be one of the best tools that can be used in evangelism in true revival. What better way to witness to people that God is real, and is real for them personally, than to receive healing and see that our God is the only true, living God?!

•

We trust this book will establish simple believing in the hearts of the people that want to follow in the steps of "a healing Jesus." The latter part of the book is filled with many testimonies of healings and miracles that we have seen and experienced.

We believe this book will inspire you to step out on your faith and pray and minister to those that have need of healing. Signs, miracles, and wonders follow those who believe and act on the promises of God!

Key: God moves when we move; just like the automatic towel dispenser when you put your hand out, and the towel comes down? When you move, God will move!

As a result, you will receive and manifest many benefits in addition to the eight we listed on the cover: Healing, Deliverance, Salvation, Power, Authority, Joy, Peace, Freedom.

2 Healing In Communion

From ancient times God has wanted healing for his people.

> ***Exodus 15:26***
> *And said, If thou wilt diligently hearken to the voice of the Lord thy God, and wilt do that which is right in his sight, and wilt give ear to his commandments, and keep all his statutes, I will put none of these diseases upon thee, which I have brought upon the Egyptians: for I am the Lord (Jehovah Rapha) that healeth thee.*

At the time Israel left Egypt, the actual first Passover was instituted. I suggest you read Exodus Chapter 12. Israel was instructed to take a male lamb without blemish and kill it on the fourteenth day of the current month. They were instructed to take the blood and strike it on the two side-posts and the upper door post (lintel). This would be their protection and preservation from the death angel.

They were to roast the lamb with fire and eat it while standing up in the night with unleavened bread and bitter herbs. Again, the blood was for protection, but as we learn from Psalms this was for healing, also.

> ***Psalms 105:37***
> *He brought them forth also with silver and gold: and there was not one feeble person among their tribes.*

Imagine, not one sick person in the whole bunch; Hallelujah! God also gave them the wealth of Egypt, did you notice that?

> ***III John 2***
> *Beloved, I wish above all things that thou mayest prosper and be in health even as thy soul prospereth.*
> ***In the Amplified Version it reads:***

> *Beloved, I pray that you may prosper in every way and (that your body) may keep well, even as (I know) your soul keeps well and prospers.*

The word *wish* can also be translated desire or prayer. Look at this--to the believer--God wants above all things that you are in health and you are not in poverty! One of the last things Jesus, in his resurrected body, said before ascending into heaven is found in Gospel of Mark.

> ***Mark 16:18***
> *They shall take up serpents; and if they drink any deadly thing, it shall not hurt them; they shall lay hands on the sick, and they shall recover.*

That *take up serpents* is the essence of *if* or *accidentally one picks up* or *runs across* a snake. Sure, there are groups of Christians that actually handle snakes and of course, eventually they get bitten, but we are not condoning stupidity.

One of the nine manifestations which is listed in I Corinthians 12, found in verse 9, is the manifestation of *gifts of healing*. Some people call

all nine manifestations "gifts", but, healing is the only manifestation that is a gift.

> ***John 14:12***
> *Verily, verily, I say unto you, He that believeth on me, the works that I do shall he do also; and greater works than these shall he do; because I go unto my Father.*

There is no time limit in this verse. The only guideline is simply believing on Jesus. So what did Jesus do? Heal and deliver! Approximately 55% of Jesus' ministry was healing and deliverance. Some people say this went out with the apostles. We are in the same period of time (administration) that was started on the day of Pentecost; the age of Grace.

This is why we named this book *God Shots*. We wanted people to understand that sometimes, healing is over time. We initiate the healing of God with prayer and sometimes by ministering or talking to specific things we know has occurred, or by things God tells us at that moment to pray for but the complete and total healing may occur over time. Just keep it simple and out of condemnation in your head. Get a God shot and move on.

Another part in healing is partaking of Holy Communion. We have seen people healed in this type of service. It may be by yourself in the privacy of your home or in your church services.

> ***Psalm 107:20***
> *He sent his word, and healed them, and delivered them from their destructions.*

See also ***Psalm 103: 1-5.***

Most people have heard about the wine representing Christ's blood for forgiveness of their sins but they have not comprehended the other element of the bread and what it represents. Just like eating the Passover lamb for health and healing, the broken bread represents the broken body of Jesus which he gave for our healing.

People understand the wine is for forgiveness of sin, but they don't understand the fullness of *by his stripes you were healed.* Look at the parallels of the Passover and Communion. Jesus as the lamb, and blood over the lintel is for our protection and preservation but, the broken body is for our healing. None of the bones in the Passover lamb or

the bones of Jesus were broken.
The lamb was complete healing for all of those who partook of the Passover lamb; 2.5 million left Egypt, with not one feeble person among them. Not even their shoes wore out!

•

I Corinthians 11:23-30 tells us about Communion, how it is done and what it represents and why it is still significant for healing, at any time.

> ***I Corinthians 11:23-30***
> *23 For I have received of the Lord that which also I delivered unto you, That the Lord Jesus the same night in which he was betrayed took bread*
> *24 And when he had given thanks he brake it, and said, Take, eat: this is my body, which is broken for you: this do in remembrance of me.*
> *25 After the same manner also he took the cup, when he had supped, saying, This cup is the new testament in my blood: this do ye, as oft as ye drink it, in remembrance of me.*
> *26 For as often as ye eat this bread, and drink this cup, ye do shew the Lord's death*

till he come.
27 Wherefore whosoever shall eat this bread, and drink this cup of the Lord unworthily, shall be guilty of the body and blood of the Lord.
28 But let a man examine himself, and so let him eat of that bread, and drink of that cup.
29 For he that eateth and drinketh unworthily, eateth and drinketh damnation to himself, not discerning the Lord's body.
30 For this cause many are weak and sickly among you, and many sleep.

In verse 27, *unworthily* means partaking but not knowing what the elements stand for. In verse 29 a better translation than *damnation* would be *consequences*. We are not trying to alter the Word to make it less powerful, we are saying this is not a good translation.

In verse 30, because many people do not know what the elements represent, many are weak and sick and many sleep (they die early or prematurely). That is why we need to know what the broken bread represents. Jesus' broken body was for our healing, glory hallelujah!

One of our favorite verses is in Hebrews 2:18. The Amplified version reads:

Hebrews 2:18
For because He Himself (in His humanity) has suffered in being tempted (tested and tried), he is able (immediately) to run to the cry of (assist, relieve) those who are being tempted and tested and tried (and who therefore are being exposed to suffering).

Jesus is ready to run to you to help you in your hour of need!

•

As we continue living in the Word, it is God's will for our lives that whatever place we are in, He wants us to continue to grow and mature. We want to take these promises and instructions in the Word and apply them in our lives for health and prosperity.

***II Peter 1:* 3-10**
3 According as his divine power hath given unto us all things that pertain unto life and

godliness, through the knowledge of him that hath called us to glory and virtue
4 Whereby are given unto us exceeding great and precious promises: that by these ye might be partakers of the divine nature, having escaped the corruption that is in the world through lust.
5 And beside this, giving all diligence, add to your faith virtue; and to virtue knowledge;
6 And to knowledge temperance patience; and to patience godliness;
7 And to godliness brotherly kindness; and to brotherly kindness charity.
8 For if these things be in you, and abound, they make you that ye shall neither be barren nor unfruitful in the knowledge of our Lord Jesus Christ.
9 But he that lacketh these things is blind, and cannot see afar off, and hath forgotten that he was purged from his old sins.
10 Wherefore the rather, brethren, give diligence to make your calling and election sure: for if ye do these things, ye shall never fall.

Well Hallelujah! We could close the book, say

Amen and all go home for chicken dinner! Some people want a formula for success, well there it is and God put a whole lot in those eight verses!
First of all, He has given us everything there is to know in life, *given* it to us, but in case you need a little something extra, there are all those things listed for us to try and do in our lives and if we do them, we have an absolute guarantee that *ye shall never fail.*

You will also notice that there are instructions for us to follow, things we are supposed to do to *make our calling and election sure.* We have our part to do. Preparing ourselves is a part of preparing to help others.

3 The Importance of Giving For Health and Healing

According to the book of Malachi, giving is very important.

> ***Malachi 3:6-10 Amplified version***
> *For I am the Lord, I change not; therefore ye sons of Jacob are not consumed. Even from the days of your fathers you have turned aside from My ordinances and have not kept them. Return to me, and I will return to you, says the Lord of hosts. But you say, How shall we return? Will a man rob or defraud God? Yet you rob and defraud Me. But you say, In what way do we rob or defraud you? You have withheld your tithes and offerings. You are cursed*

with the curse, for you are robbing Me, even this whole nation.
Bring me all the this (the whole tenth of your income) *into the storehouse, that there may be food in My house, and prove Me now by it, says the Lord of hosts, if I will not open the windows of heaven for you and pour you out a blessing, that there shall not be room enough to receive it.*
And I will rebuke the devourer (the devil) *for your sakes and he shall not destroy the fruits of our ground, neither shall your vine drop its fruit before the time in the field, says the Lord of hosts. And all nations shall call you happy and blessed, for you shall be a land of delight, says the Lord of hosts.*

There are those that teach that we are not under the law, which is true. However, giving of ten percent was established before the law was given. After Abram (before God changed his name to Abraham), returned from the slaughter of Chedorlaomer; Melchizedek (which means King of Righteousness) , King of Salem, who was also the Priest of the Most High, was given tithes by Abram. See Genesis 14:12-20.

Now we know that Jesus was a priest after the order of Melchizedek which lends credence to the tithe still being established. Remember that Malachi 3:6 states that the Lord changes not. Verse 11 states "*And I will rebuke the devourer* (the devil) *for your sakes*."

This is important to your health, well-being and prosperity. The word *tithe* means "Tenth". Hebrews 7:1-9 establishes the superiority of Melchizedek priesthood to the Levites. Jesus Christ, who arose as High Priest, continually bears the likeness of Melchizedek. The Levites who received tithes virtually paid them through Abraham to Melchizedek. Abraham is still the Father of Faith for all those that believe whether we adhere to the 10% or give more as a love offering. By grace, you pick one. We cannot out-give God.

We are convinced that we should give at least ten percent to God because we have done it, and we know that it works! We also need to remember that God said *tithes and offerings* and so they are not identical and we need not short-change God in either category. Can it also mean time and service in the body? Surely, but we cannot substitute that for financial giving.

If you are struggling with financial abundance and not having any, this is indicative that you are not giving enough. Luke 6:38 and many other scriptures tell us that when we give, we will have more, not less.

People want a Savior but they don't want a Lord, especially when it comes to money! Many wealthy people don't even think they need God because of their wealth but God is very specific about finances and people can miss the boat and wonder why they are having difficulties.

Mike: I taught in a home church on giving and receiving until I was blue in the face, how important it was. Now this one couple, they finally they put in $150 one week and that was pretty much the end of it. They came to me and said they needed help so I asked "Well what's the problem?" "Well", he said, "It didn't work" (giving) but then a few minutes later the husband said "I went to the dentist and they knocked $1500 off the bill"; ten times what he gave but he didn't see it. He didn't see it! I call it the spirit of slumber; he totally could not see the benefits.

Judi: Our IRS audit story... What a miracle that was! Well, you know, we live part-time in Ohio, part-time in Florida. While we were in Ohio, the IRS had been sending us notices in Florida and we didn't know it until we returned to Florida. Mike opened a piece of mail from the IRS advising us we had back taxes due in the amount of $460,000! I opened another piece that contained penalties of $90,000 for lack of a 10-day response to the original letter for a total due of $550,000!! The natural man in me started thinking that we were about to lose everything, we would have to sell everything! Mike said not to worry about it but I did not get much sleep that night; as you can imagine, it was very unnerving.

Mike: I called the local Sarasota IRS office for an appointment and the woman we spoke to on the phone did not sound well. Though I thought we should probably pray for her, we did not, but we agreed to meet in about three-weeks-time.

Judi was on the other phone and had the same feeling that I did; that we should have prayed for the agent. The next morning as I showered I asked God if we should pray for this lady at the IRS office and He gave me one word; "Publican". In the Bible, Publican represented a tax collector. This one word so resounded with me that I felt that we should contact the agent.

Judi and I each got on a phone and when the lady answered, I told her that she was probably going to think that we're nuts, but God wanted us to pray for her. We told her we were both ministers and that we pray for people and they get healed. We prayed for her sinuses and allergies and asked if there was anything else she needed prayer for and she said yes, for her son.

In Judi's spirit, she knew the son's problem was depression but she did not acknowledge that. We prayed for the woman's son and agreed to meet in three weeks. We checked with our CPA who had advised us that there were no problems in the way we had been filing our taxes, and returned for the appointment. While we were in the office, the IRS agent pulled out a tax book that had to be three inches thick and read some regulations out of it. Our CPA was wrong and the IRS agent was right! I believe God sent this lady as an angel to take care of our tax problem.

She was the most delightful lady and proceeded to

help us in every way that she could. There were times that she would ask us "Why didn't you take this deduction?" and I told her that I didn't know that we could or should, so we spent several days a week for almost three months going over tax issues.

We got the taxes due down to $80 or $90,000, then down to $40,000 and finally down to about $10-11,000. That sure was a long ways from $550,000! When it hit about $10,000, I said "That's it for me" but she said there were still receipts on the credit card transfer papers, and though they can fade over time, if I went through all of my credit card information, I might be able to reduce that amount even more.

We also told her that we were ministers and we would appreciate it if she could speed up the results to allow us to move about the country to make our commitments without this burden upon us. It was about three months later that I received a call from the agent telling me that she was going to "Make my day". She said we owed $2,530 and I said "Hallelujah, praise the Lord!" She asked, "What did you say?" I repeated what I said and she said she would be sending me the papers showing the amount owed and if I agreed, to sign the papers and return them with a check.

I was thrilled with the amount that was owed but 15 minutes later, I received another call stating that when she was about ready to slip that in an envelope something else came to mind and she put some information in the computer. She asked, "What do you think that amount is now?" I had no idea. It was zero! Can you believe that! Glory, Hallelujah, Praise the Lord!!! God the Father and His Son, Jesus, and the Holy Spirit, and many angels must have been operating in this situation. What a blessing! God is good all the time!

•

There is an idiom regarding monetary arrangements with other nations found in ***Deuteronomy 28: 12-13*** which tells us we will be the greatest nation and not the least nation so our individual giving has an impact on the nation. We also have blessings that ***will come on thee and overtake thee*** stated in that same chapter, thus we give so that we may also personally receive.

Luke 6:38

Give and it shall be given unto you good measure, pressed down, and shaken together, and running over, shall men give into your bosom. For with the same measure that ye mete withal it shall be measured to you again.

III John:2 Amplified Version
Beloved, I pray that you may prosper in every way and (that your body) may keep well, even as (I know) your soul keeps well and prosper.

If you are having financial difficulty, it may be because you feel you cannot give or, give to God first. We can argue about how much and when or if we should at all, but if you are going to all the trouble to argue, the truth is probably working on you. We want to mature in our walk, so that is something to think about.

•

From Mike's 2010 teaching on CD

Once you start giving the right proportion and to the right place, then you start claiming and declaring your prosperity.

You speak to your wallet, your billfold or your checking account! (*Thunk—is the sound of his wallet hitting the table)*

> ***Mark 11: 23 & 24***
> *For verily I say unto you, that whoever shall say unto this mountain, Be thou removed, and shall not doubt in his heart, but shall believe that those things which he saith shall come to pass; he shall have whatsoever he said. Therefore I say unto you, what things soever ye desire, when ye pray, believe that ye receive them, and ye shall have them.*

You think I'm crazy, don't you? Well, you speak to that checking account, you speak to it, you expect God to bless it, you claim it in the name of Jesus Christ! Not long ago, I was looking at my checking account and there was $8,600 that appeared. I'm asking myself, it's from the government, so I don't question it?

Ha! It's from the government, they'll take it back! Anyway, I'm looking at the $8,600 and finally I get a note that says they overcharged me from 2004, 2005, 2006, 2007. They overcharged me some $2,200 a year on Social Security but they gave it back to me. We see blessings like this in our lives all the time.

•

There are times in our lives... Did I tell about Judi modeling? She tells everyone she did not model and I said "Judi, you're making a liar out of me!" Well, there was a rack of clothes at a particular store and there was announcement "For the next five minutes, all these clothes on this rack are a dollar each" and it wasn't K-Mart either! Judi bought things for herself and for our daughter. Judi wore one of the dollar outfits to the modeling show and all the ladies said afterwards "We like those clothes but we like what you are wearing the best" and it was a buck! God just gives to us, as we've been giving. He's just been multiplying it back to us.

•

Oh, that part in ***Deuteronomy 28: 2*** that tells us "*And all these blessings shall come on thee and* *overtake thee..."* We know a gal has recently had a former employer from four years ago that sent her a check in the mail when she updated her address for tax purposes. They said *"It is not for the 401 account but we've been trying to track you down to give you this money."*

•

Do you want to be a receiver of God's goodness? Well, you have to be a giver of God's goodness. You have to be willing to release your hold on your money, plain and simple.

II Corinthians 9 (all of the chapter has some powerful keys) but verse 10 says *"Now he that ministereth seed to the sower both minister bread for your food, and multiply your seed sown, and increase the fruits of your righteousness."*

He gives seed to whom? The sower.

The man or woman who is humble and meek enough to do what God tells them to do; get rid of it, will get the benefit and reward for having done it. He will give them the seed money and keep giving to the one who will broadcast it, spread it around!

Who do we give to besides the church, as a group?

> ***Galatians 6:10***
> *As we have therefore opportunity, let us do good unto all men, especially unto them who are of the household of faith.*

We want to make sure we are taking care of our brethren in the household first, not after every other 'cause' in the community, excluding the household. When we hear about someone having a need and have the means to give, that is our instruction in Acts 4: 32-37. It benefits the body of Christ when we follow through, as well as the individual.

> ***Acts 2:33***
> *And with great power gave the apostles witness of the resurrection of the Lord Jesus: and great grace was upon them all.*

We want to be sure we have the skills to "*Owe no man anything, but to love one another: for he that loveth another hath fulfilled the law.*" ***(Romans 13:8)*** If we owe money on everything then we need to stop living above our means. We should stop ignoring that we need to give! We also need to save for a time when we don't want or cannot work every day of our lives.

There are plenty of teachings and classes on financial stewardship; good Christian-based information, to teach us how to get out of debt and start saving. Doing it is up to us.

If we are to owe no man anything then we need to think about how we manage large purchases, build homes and build churches.

It ***does*** take money in our culture to do things, if it is not a gift and not a barter for services but, also, God wants us to *prosper and be in health.* Some people say "Oh that was just for spiritual wealth" but God does want us to have spiritual growth and vitality. Money and financial wholeness are a part of God's desire for us.

> ***Deuteronomy 8:17 & 18***
> *And thou say in thine heart, My power and the might of mine hand hath gotten me this wealth. But thou shalt remember the Lord thy God: for it is He that given thee power*

to get wealth, that he may establish his covenant which he sware unto thy fathers as it is this day.

Psalms 112:1-3

1 Praise ye the Lord. Blessed is the man that feareth the Lord, that delighteth greatly in his commandments.
2 His seed shall be mighty upon earth: the generation of the upright shall be blessed.
3 Wealth and riches shall be in his house: and his righteousness endureth for ever.

Since it is to the church of Grace, Galatians 6:6-9 is specifically about giving and receiving. It is an instruction to us. Do we want God's perspective and ways of handling money and wealth?

If our heart is right, we should do as we are in instructed in Ephesians:

Ephesians 4:28

Let him that stole, steal no more; but rather let him labour, working with his hands the thing which is good, that he may have to give to him that needeth.

God Shots

This is one of the main purposes of our lives: we are to work to give to people that have a need.

4 Kingdom Living

The Word speaks a lot about kingdoms. There are three different kingdoms; two are rather large and one, rather small. ***Luke 12:31 says*:**

> ***Luke 12:31***
> *But rather, seek ye the kingdom of God; and all these things shall be added unto you.*

See also ***Matthew 6:33.***

God is talking about all the things that you need in your life, but he also says that He will give us the desires of our heart.

> ***Psalm 37:4***
> *Delight thyself also in the Lord; and he*

shall give thee the desires of thine heart.

The kingdom we should seek is God's kingdom. The adversary, the devil, satan, also has a kingdom. The third kingdom is our own selves. The kingdom that resides in our mind; the one that says we are King and Lord over our lives. We can see and listen to all three of these kingdoms but the kingdom of God is the one that we need to live in. The Word of God says that we are to reign as Kings and priests.

We want to self-direct our hearts and minds to kingdom living in the best kingdom and when we do that, God will bless us with not only the things of sustenance that we need, but in addition to those, we can be living a kingly life and a life with the deepest desires of our heart, ***if*** we put Him and our search for ***His*** kingdom first.

Philippians 3:19-21

19 Whose end is destruction, whose God is their belly, and whose glory is in their shame, who mind earthly things.

20 For our conversation is in heaven; from whence also we look for the Savior, the Lord Jesus Christ:

21 Who shall change our vile body, that it may be fashioned like unto his glorious body, according to the working whereby he is able even to subdue all things unto himself.

In verse 20, the word "conversation" is actually "citizenship". We have a Commonwealth, a heavenly origin. We are not only in the Commonwealth but, we have *common wealth.* As sons of God and of the King, we are entitled to the same resources as the King.

Westerners have a difficult time with "kingdom" living, because here in the United States, we live in a Democracy; actually, it is a Republic. We have a Constitution and under this system, man is always making changes.

In a kingdom, there is a King. He makes the rules or law. What the King says, that's it. The culture is also impacted by what the King, or top-ranking monarch in the country, adopts as a custom. In the United Kingdom, when the Queen has tea at a particular time of day, the citizens also have tea. As we choose to live in the Kingdom of God in our minds, then we reap the inheritance equally with the Lord Jesus Christ. We have it, spiritually speaking, but we may not be living it because we are allowing something else to be Lord in our lives.

Romans 8:17
And if children, then heirs; heirs of God, and joint-heirs with Christ; if so be that we suffer with him that we may be also glorified together.

Ephesians 1:11
In whom also we have obtained an inheritance, being predestinated according to the purpose of him who worketh all things after the counsel of his own will.

This is why we want to continue to seek that kingdom. God has withheld nothing from us. We are on the same legal ground as the Lord Jesus Christ, a joint-heir! Hallelujah! Another aspect of God's kingdom living are the resources and benefits that are available to us from the kingdom.

Matthew 5:7-12
7 Blessed are the merciful: for they shall obtain mercy.

> *8 Blessed are the pure in heart: for they shall see God.*
> *9 Blessed are the peacemakers: for they shall be called the children of God.*
> *10 Blessed are they which are persecuted for righteousness' sake: for theirs is the kingdom of heaven.*
> *11 Blessed are ye, when men shall revile you, and persecute you, and shall say all manner of evil against you falsely, for my sake.*
> *12 Rejoice, and be exceeding glad: for great is your reward in heaven: for so persecuted they the prophets which were before you.*

We are in a contest, a spiritual warfare between the two kingdoms but, with the kingdom of God, comes great power and authority.

> **I John 4:4b ...***because greater is he that is in you, than he* (satan) *that is in the world.*

When Jesus sent for the twelve, he commanded them in Matthew 10:7, "*And as ye go, preach, saying, The kingdom of heaven is at hand* (has arrived). *Heal the sick, cleanse the lepers, raise the dead, cast out devils: freely ye have received, freely give."* How about them apples? This is what we have as the King's kids and this is what we should be doing as the King's kids!

•

Society trains us to be a servant. We are trained to get a job. In God's kingdom, He wants you to be trained to be a leader. Actually, every person born again of God's Spirit is a leader. Everyone is designed to be a leader in his own gift.

Leadership has to be more than in our job, but also in our marriage. I could be a CEO with a multi-million dollar business, but lose my marriage or children. We have to be able to be a leader and manager our marriage and family. We should minister first to our own home, and then we can take it to the people on the streets. Our home and family is our little kingdom, but an important one. In this little kingdom, our focus should be on God's kingdom and the Father, *Abba*. ("Abba" meaning, Father or Daddy: our source and sustainer.) Just as God is our *Abba*, we as fathers need to be *Abbas* to our family, and yet, we need to be in constant communication with the Father. Do not have the idea that we can do everything on our own.

When we get away from that personal relationship with the Father and his Son, we turn Christianity into a religion. The Word says we are to have fellowship; *koinōnia* is the Greek word, with God and with Jesus, otherwise, we are practicing a religion. A definition of religion is *the worship of a deity through a set of beliefs expressed through rituals and customs.* Good news! A kingdom is not of religion; a kingdom is a country governed by a king with all the components of a nation's citizens having power.

> **Matthew 4:17**
> *From that time Jesus began to preach, and to say, Repent: for the kingdom of heaven is at hand* (has arrived).

Jesus Christ didn't come to set up a religion, he came to set up a kingdom. We need to repent—change our minds—from this concept of religion, and instead, live the concept of citizenship in a country or kingdom, having fellowship with the King. Well Amen!

The theology of the 20th and 21st century Church is

not the principal theology of the Bible. Martin Luther finally came along and confronted the Roman Catholic Church; that it was by grace that we are saved and not by works and that the just shall live by faith.

The kingdom concept is **the** foundation of all scripture and revelation. The kingdom concept is necessary for correct interpretation and application of scripture. The kingdom concepts are the main subject throughout Scripture and provides the foundation for understanding the motivation, purpose, plans and actions of God. Without the kingdom concept, Biblical understanding and theology is defective.

•

God uses different ways of calling attention to things in the Bible; Figures of Speech, repetitions, parenthetical phrases or in different styles of writing to let something be known. A parable is designed to hide truth until it is time for the truth to be revealed and received. Matthew 13:1-11 is the well-known parable of the "sower and the seed".

Matthew 13:1-11

1 The same day went Jesus out of the house, and sat by the sea side.

2 And great multitude were gathered together unto him, so that he went into a ship, and sat; and the whole multitude stood on the shore.

3 And he spake many things unto them in parables, saying, Behold, a sower went forth to sow;

4 And when he sowed, some seeds fell by the way side, and the fowls came and devoured them up:

5 Some fell upon stony places, where they had not much earth: and forthwith they sprung up, because they had no deepness of earth:

6 And when the sun was up, they were scorched; and because they had no root, they withered away.

7 And some fell among thorns; and the thorns sprung up, and choked them:

8 But other fell into good ground, and brought forth fruit, some an hundredfold, some sixty fold, some thirty fold.

9 Who hath ears to hear, let him hear.

10 And the disciples came, and said unto

him, Why speakest thou unto them in parables?
11 He answered and said unto them, Because it is given unto you to know the mysteries of the kingdom of heaven, but to them it is not given.

God does not sow any bad seed. Some people do not really want to know the truth and Jesus knew that. God only wants to fill those who hunger. God is everywhere but He only reveals Himself to those that want him and seek after Him and His kingdom.

Matthew 13:12-15
12 For whosoever hath, to him shall be given, and he shall have more abundance: but whosoever hat not, from him shall be taken away even that he hath.
13 Therefore speak I to them in parables: because they seeing see not; and hearing they hear not, neither do they understand.
14 And in them is fulfilled the prophecy of Esaias, which said, By hearing ye shall hear, and shall not understand; and seeing ye shall see, and shall not perceive:
15 For this people's heart is waxed gross,

and their ears are dull of hearing, and their eyes they have closed; lest at any time they should see with their eyes and hear with their ears, and should understand with their heart, and should be converted, and I should heal them.

Their eyes are closed! Ignorance due to being uniformed is not the same as choosing to be ignorant. Self-imposed ignorance is the height of stupidity. Because we live in this kingdom, prosperity and wealth come with the kingdom. If you remember the exodus of Israel from Egypt, the Word says there was no person "feeble" person among them. Another translation in the Hebrew for "feeble" is "pauper". They were all rich because they brought the wealth of Egypt with them. God made this provision for them in the kingdom. Read Matthew 13:16 & 17. We have heard more than Moses, David and all of the Old Testament prophets.

Matthew 13:16 & 17

Blessed are your eyes, for they see: and your ears, for they hear. For verily I say unto you, that many prophets and righteous men have desired to see those things which ye see, and have not seen them; and to hear those things which ye hear, and have not heard them.

Being born-again into the kingdom is not a religious experience, but a *citizenship* and *kingdom* experience. When we state Romans 10:9 & 10, saying Jesus is our Lord and Savior now, and believe that He is the Son of God and that God raised him from the dead, this statement to God makes us whole; with body, soul and spirit, legally connecting us to God again. At that very moment, we receive son-ship by seed of the Almighty God! That expression *born again* that we hear frequently of a religious experience, literally means in the Greek; *anothen*, born from above.

I Peter 1:23
Being born again not of corruptible seed, but incorruptible, by the word of God, which liveth and abideth for ever.

We are born of God's seed, incorruptible and with it, come all the rights and privileges of the son of God!
In contrast, are we so committed to our religion, to our church, to our Pastor, that we sometimes reject

the Word of God? In many churches traditions, rituals, customs, rites, and wrong beliefs have replaced the simple truths of God's Word and His Kingdom.

We need to be cautious of letting one or two men or women determine what they claim the rightly divided Word of God says. We need to get to the point in our lives where we can determine through working it ourselves, and through the Holy Spirit, what the Word is saying to us. We know what the Word is saying to us in this day and time.

> ***John 14:26***
> *But the Comforter, which is the Holy Spirit, whom the father will send in my name, he shall teach you all things, and bring all things to your remembrance, whatsoever I have said unto you.*
>
> ***Amplified Version*** *But the Comforter (Counselor, Helper, Intercessor, Advocate, Strengthener, Standby), the Holy Spirit, Whom the Father will send in My name (in My place to represent Me and act on My behalf), He will teach you all things. And He will cause you to recall (will remind*

you of, bring to your remembrance) everything I have told you.

God is able to lead us to the truth of His Word. Sure, God has given us teachers, but we need to check to make sure that what is being taught is the truth and that it is rightly-divided. I don't think that if we all sit down and read the Word in a given passage, that we would all come out with the same answer, and I do not think that is all wrong, either. Because of the complexity of the Greek and Hebrew languages, the words have many meanings. Add in the orientalisms, customs of the Bible times, and figures of speech, it becomes a lifetime of study. Nevertheless, it behooves us to do as II Timothy 2:15 states:

II Timothy 2:15
Study to show thyself approved unto God, a workman that needeth not to be ashamed, rightly dividing the word of *truth.*

There can be fresh, new revelation at our fingertips on a daily basis!

5 The Dream And Vision

Mike: At around the age of eight, I was taken to Sunday School by my Aunt May and Uncle Bill. I was deeply touched by the teaching that day. The lady teaching the lesson taught about how Jesus, Paul and Peter healed the sick, blind and lame. That night as I lie in my bed, I told God that I would like to do that.

I just remember that the tears streamed down as I visualized that dream for myself. To think a person, other than someone in the Bible, would be able to that! As far as I know, no one in the church was healing anyone; at least I never heard of it.

I really didn't think much more about it until another 28 years. At the age of 36, I started to really get into the Word. That is when things started to happen supernaturally to me and to my wife, Judi. This started us on a quest for more of God and everything available that the Father and His son, Jesus, made available.

When a person gets to a point that they want to seek the things of God, God will open doors for them.

> ***Matthew 7: 7 & 8***
> *Ask, and it shall be given you; seek, and ye shall find; knock, and it shall be opened unto you: For every one that asketh receiveth; and he that seeketh findeth; and to him that knocketh it shall be opened.*

We started listening and visiting programs and teachings of people who have active healing ministries and along the way, we would talk to people and offer to pray with them. We had a prophecy from Pastor Billie Burke that we had a healing ministry; both of us, and, that it would take place in parking lots, airports, grocery stores, and churches. This has turned out to be true. We had been doing those very things but this further confirmed what God had us doing.

The thing to remember is that all Christians born again (Romans 10:9 & 10) have the same power as Christ and what they do with it, is up to them.

We were healing and doing things long before we became Ordained in service as Christian Ministers but we have included the prophecy from our ordination so that you can see that God will tell you what He has planned for you and what God's desire for your future is for answering His call.

Our Ordination Prophecy:

I've called you to preach the gospel of Jesus Christ concerning the great mystery, to win people for Me. To proclaim My power and deliverance, to turn them from darkness to life, from the power of satan unto Me, to open to them a knowledge of who My son is and what he's done for them. To bring the light of the gospel of deliverance, so go out and preach and heal, and deliver. I've called you to heal My people and to bring before them My Word. That they know it's available right here and right now. That I'm a God who delivers with might and miracles and power, so never be afraid to speak for Me.

God Shots

Cast down the imaginations and the thinking of lack, for I am a God who provides exceeding, abundantly above all that you could ask or think, and I have doors open for you to walk through. I have a path of richness, a path of great miracles before you. So walk through them, walk into this great field of abundance and bring My people there and deliver them, with healing and with My Word. This great mystery is that I live within all of you, so do it together and lead My people to victory.

As you can see, besides healing and deliverance, God has called us to preach the gospel of Jesus Christ concerning the Great Mystery and to win people for the Lord and, salvation is the greatest healing, ever!

6 Forgiveness

Forgiveness is very effectual in healing and particularly, in deliverance ministering. If Judi or I know that we are going to be ministering to a person, we ask them to make a list of people that they think they have to forgive. Once they make the list, we instruct them to forgive the people on the list. It does not have to be be done publicly.

> ***Mark 11:23-26***
> *23 For verily I say unto you, That whosoever shall say unto this mountain, Be thou removed, and be thou cast into the sea; and shall not doubt in his heart, but shall believe that those things which he saith shall come to pass; he shall have whatsoever he saith.*

24 Therefore I say unto you, What things soever ye desire, when ye pray, believe that ye receive them, and ye shall have them.
25 And when ye stand praying, forgive, if ye have ought against any: that your Father also which is in heaven forgive your trespasses.

I like the Amplified Version of Mark 11:25.

Mark 11:25
And whenever you stand praying, if you have anything against anyone, forgive him and let it drop—leave it, let it go—in order that your Father who is in heaven may also forgive you your (own) *failings and shortcomings and let them drop.*

We know that people have suffered through a lot of harm, damage and evil, or, perhaps committed it, but unforgiveness can be a stumbling block; an obstacle, to receiving total deliverance. We may have to just say it with the best heart that we can and tell God *"Help thou my unbelief!"* because we have been wronged, perhaps even been made to be a victim, repeatedly. However, we do not want that unforgiveness to grow to be a root of bitterness, allowing it to stay and come back on us. The Word tells us to *let it drop*, so there must be a way to do this. How many of our marriages and relationships would be better if we would do this a little more often?

> ***Hebrews 12:15***
> *Looking diligently lest any man fail of the grace of God; lest any root of bitterness springing up trouble you, and thereby many be defiled.*

> ***Proverbs 14:10-14***
> ***10*** *The heart knoweth his own bitterness; and a stranger doth not intermeddle with his joy.*
> *11 The house of the wicked shall be overthrown: but the tabernacle of the upright shall flourish.*
> *12 There is a way which seemeth right unto a man, but the end thereof are the ways of death.*
> *13 Even in laughter the heart is sorrowful; and the end of that mirth is heaviness.*
> *14 The backslider in heart shall be filled with his own ways: and a good man shall be satisfied from himself.*

Sometimes forgiving people is a very difficult thing to do and the reasons for the bitterness and anger may be very legitimate and private. However, stating aloud that you forgive the person or people in the situations, can break the hold of the devil. He likes to trespass but we belong to Jesus. He brought us back from the clutches of the adversary. We have been bought with a price and the price was the shed blood and broken body of Jesus on the cross at Calvary. He paid the price for any forgiveness; we declare it.

Reverend Joyce Meyer has an excellent book on the bondage of bitterness and rejection and how to break them off of your life; *The Root of Rejection.* Peter asked Jesus how many times should he forgive a person that sinned against him and Jesus replied in Matthew 18.

> ***Matthew 18:21 & 22***
> *Then came Peter to him, and said, Lord, how oft shall my brother sin against me, and I forgive him? Till seven times? Jesus saith unto him, I say not unto thee, Until seven times: but, Until seventy times seven.*

Forgiveness is extended, not because we finally get to the place where we think the person may be worthy, it is given because it is required of us. Only you can answer the question *Is there someone?* If there is; yourself or others, take steps to get this taken care of.

What if that person is already dead? Well, that would be a question for yourself, also. Does what that person did still have a hold, still have impact on your life, routinely? Sometimes, we have reminders that come up because of an event, which may be associated with a particular date or time of year, but, if they are not something we think about on a routine basis, it is like a scar in the mind. It is there, you are reminded but it doesn't hurt any more, you have moved on. If you have not, seek help.

Also, let us not forget forgiveness of ourselves. One thing that comes up before ministering to a person is that sometimes, they feel they are unworthy to receive healing, particularly in the area of deliverance. This unforgiveness of self are the feelings of guilt and unworthiness.

Jesus Christ went to the cross and shed every drop

of His blood for our remission and forgiveness of sin. "*All* (Everyone*) have sinned and come short of the glory of God,"* **(Romans 3:23.)**

We may not feel like we deserve the Lord's forgiveness but that is beside the point. The Word says we are entitled to it. We may be so humbled and thankful that we are! ***Romans 8:1*** is a familiar verse, but we also like in the Amplified Version of I John 3:20-22.

I John 3:20-22

20 Whenever our hearts in tormenting self-accusation make us feel guilty and condemn us, (For we are in God's hands), For He is above and greater than our consciences (our hearts), and He knows (perceives and understands) everything (nothing is hidden from Him).

21 And, beloved, if our consciences (our hearts) do not accuse (if they do not make us feel guilty and condemn us) we have confidence (complete assurance and boldness) before God.

22 And we receive from Him whatever we ask, because we (watchfully) obey His orders (observe His suggestions and injunctions, follow His plan for us) and (habitually) practice what is pleasing to Him.

Folks, God has thought of everything our brain or his adversary might throw at us to keep us away from the throne where grace, mercy and forgiveness abide. Condemnation and guilt are two of the hardest bookends to topple. They will keep us from asking and expecting to receive anything from God. In addition, we do not approach the throne of God inching our way forward as worms. NO! He has already made us acceptable through Christ, *"holy and without blame before him in love,"* (***Ephesians 1:4)*** so you know what we do?

Hebrews 4:16
Let us therefore come boldly unto the throne of grace, that we may obtain mercy, and find grace to help in time of need.

Boldly we go and ask for our needs and the needs of others to be met. Actually, we can command them to be, in the name of Jesus. In addition, you may be surprised to see that in several places in the Word, others have and we may, remind God of His specific promises attached to our need which also helps remind us, that He has likely delivered us several times before and is still at work now, willing to do of His good pleasure toward us. It may not be in our time table, but, God is at work. How do we know this?

> ***I John 1:5***
> *This then is the message which we have heard of him, and declare unto you, that God is light, and in him is no darkness at all.*

Simply stated, God is good, all the time; without exception. That has to mean that sickness, disease and death come from some other source, and now, God has revealed even that to us. Attributions to God killing and "smiting" (particularly in the Old Testament) are not going to be handled here, but in most large Concordances, you can look up references in the front or appendices about *idioms of permission* and that will get you started.

It takes God working in a man or woman's heart to come to a knowledge of the truth. The Gospel of John reveals:

John 14:16-18

*16 And I will pray the Father, and he shall
give you another Comforter, that may
abide with you forever
17 Even the spirit of truth; whom the world
cannot receive, because it seeth him not,
neither knoweth him: but ye know him; for
he dwelleth with you and shall be in you.
18 I will not leave you comfortless: I will
come to you.*

7 Salvation & The Mystery

These two components of Christianity have been a "mystery" in most denominations for centuries. In fact, it is most likely why we have so many denominations. One group does not agree with the other on certain doctrines, so they split off and make their way of doing things the way they feel is "the right way".

To a certain degree, we all do that; we will know for sure when the Lord returns but, if we go to God's Word and let it speak for itself, most of those opposing views will fall away. The Bible interprets itself either in the verse, how it was used before in the Bible, or, within the context that the verse appears.

God had to make it easy for us, and He has. Most of this; though you can spend a lifetime on it, is so simple, a child can read and believe it. Salvation (wholeness now and eternal life later) is for anyone who wants it but here is a tip: not everyone is going to want it, in fact, it is *"foolishness unto them"* I Corinthians 1:18 & 21.

However, there are probably a lot of people, who, if they really saw the goodness of God and the evilness of the devil, would pick God's way. We never stop praying for people, for their hearts to change and for them to see their own need for God, but, we really understand that all people do not want God.

This book is not directed to you, though if you have it, that means someone has not given up on you, for eternity, is a long time! Perhaps you have your own theology or history on what you think the Bible says, but, for a few pages, put that aside. Put everything you ever heard in neutral and read on.

Salvation is being saved from sin unto everlasting life, deliverance, healing, soundness, wholeness, preservation, peace, security, safety, peace and freedom from all works of the enemy (the devil). Young's Analytical Concordance states it as *soundness, safety and peace.* Well who doesn't want those things in their life?

***Does a person need to be born again to be healed?* No.**

***Does a Person need to be born again to minister healing?* Yes.**

One needs to be born again and filled with the holy spirit to operate the power and authority that Jesus Christ has delivered unto us. It may be unknown to you at the moment you are praying, but if you want an active healing ministry that is not hit-and-miss, yes, you have to know that you are born-again and have the power to work with. First, let us look at what "Born again" really means.

> ***Romans 10:9 & 10***
> *That if thou shalt confess with thy mouth the Lord Jesus, and shalt believe in thine heart that God hath raised him from the dead, thou shalt be saved. For with the heart man believeth unto righteousness; and with the mouth confession is made*

unto salvation.

We confess Jesus as our Lord; the Greek word is *kurios*, meaning Lord, Master, Sir. In other words, the Boss! Jesus is the Boss!

When it says to confess, does that mean listing all of your sins to an audience? No. It means to declare Christ is the boss, He alone is the Savior. He paid the price of your salvation with his life, not by you reciting everything bad that you can remember about yourself. You can declare that out loud just between you and God, anywhere. If you would like to make it public, that is up to you. ***You declare Christ is the Savior,*** not your sins and your sinful nature!

The moment you make this confession of Jesus as Lord, he comes into your heart and the greatest miracle and healing you will ever experience, will take place. You will have what Colossians 1:27 refers to as "*Christ in you, the hope of glory.*" Not only do you receive remission and forgiveness of sin, but you have everlasting life; WOW!

II Corinthians 4:7

But we have this treasure in earthen

vessels, that the excellency of the power may be of God, and not of us.

What a truth; that we have God in Christ dwelling in us and the power that lives in us is not of ourselves, but of God; Oh Hallelujah!

II Corinthians 5:17
Therefore if any man is be in Christ, he a new creature: old things are passed away; behold, all things are become new.

I like the Amplified Version even better:

II Corinthians 5:17
Therefore, if any person is (ingrafted) in Christ (the Messiah) he is a new creation (a new creature altogether); the old (previous moral and spiritual condition) has passed away. Behold, the fresh and new has come!

Yes, we have a new start, a new life! We have been moved out of darkness into the glorious light of the Father and his son, Jesus Christ. We are born from above; from God's spirit which is placed inside of us, never to be lost! It is God in

Christ in us. Hallelujah!! Amazing!

Some people think this being born again is too easy. Well, it is too easy! Jesus made it easy. He paid the price. He was beaten, shed his precious blood, hung on a cross and was buried, but then, the Father raised him from the grave. Do you get it? Jesus paid the price, not by works that we do. We are saved by grace! Amazing Grace!

> ***Ephesians 2:8*** *For by grace are ye saved through faith; and that not of yourselves: it is the gift of God.*

Some people would ask *What difference does it make?* Well, it makes ***all*** the difference because it is literally, the power of Christ, in us and ***that*** was hidden. ***That*** was part of the **mystery**; not that we have to figure out why God does what He does or does not do, or what did I do wrong, or what did I do right? No! *The Mystery* is what God kept a secret; kept it hidden until Jesus fulfilled the laws with his death and resurrection. He rose again to make available that power to us, who do one thing: ***believe.***

Ephesians 3: 1-6, & 9
1 For this cause I Paul, the prisoner of Jesus Christ for you Gentiles,
2 If ye have heard of the dispensation of the grace of God which is given me to you-ward:
3 How that by revelation he made known unto me the mystery; (as I wrote afore in few words,
4 Whereby, when ye read, ye may understand my knowledge in the mystery of Christ)
5 Which in other ages was not made known unto the sons of men, as it is now revealed unto his holy apostles and prophets by the Spirit;
6 That the Gentiles should be fellowheirs, and of the same body, and partakers of his promise in Christ by the gospel...
9 And make all men see what is the fellowship of the mystery, which from the beginning of the world hath been hid in God, who created all things by Jesus Christ.

This *great mystery* in verse 6 brought the Gentiles

into the fold; the family of God. Colossians 1:27 sheds more light on it.

Colossians 1:27
To whom God would make known what is the riches of the glory of this mystery among the Gentiles; which is ***Christ in you, the hope of glory.***

There was no reference in any previous scriptures about this. God had this concealed in His bosom. For the first time in history, the Gentiles would be fellow-heirs with God and joint-heirs with Christ.

I Corinthians 2:7 & 8
But we speak the wisdom of God in a mystery, even the hidden wisdom, which God ordained before the world unto our glory: Which none of the princes of this world knew: for had they known it, they would not have crucified the Lord of glory.

Ephesians 1:19 & 20 *And what is the exceeding greatness of his power to usward who believe, according to the working of his mighty power Which he wrought in Christ, when he raised him* *from the dead, and set him at his own right hand in the heavenly places.*

This is so powerful! Had the devil known this, he never would have had Jesus crucified. Why? Because there was only one Jesus on earth but when Christ chose to fulfill the law on all points to be our redeemer and Savior and was then raised from the dead, the rulership of the devil was smashed!

If you only take one thing away from this book, take this: *Jesus could only be in one place at one time. Now, wherever a believer is, they have the power and authority to do the works that Jesus did, and more: "and greater works shall ye do for I go unto my father."* ***(John 14:12)***

Taking away that much is a game-changer for you, the rest of your life!

Salvation is available for those who what? Give a bunch of cash, confess sins, try to be perfect, quit cursing and taking God's name in vain? No, simply by believing and declaring Jesus as the Lord in your life as we see in Romans 10:9 & 10. We have written it before but we want you to see it again:

Romans 10:9 & 10 Amplified Version:
Because if you acknowledge and confess with your lips that Jesus is Lord and in your heart believe (adhere to, trust in and rely on the truth) that God raised him from the dead, you will be saved. For with the heart a person believes (adheres to, trusts in and relies on Christ), and so is justified (declared righteous, acceptable to God), and with the mouth he confesses (declares openly and speaks out freely his faith) and confirms (his) salvation.

This then would explain why Jesus declared at his Crucifixion, "*For this purpose was I spared*" though those words in Aramaic that are translated other ways. God did **not** forsake His only begotten son. Jesus knew He was the propitiation, the payment, that had to be made for all of us to have what we have available today, and he *gave* his life, he was not killed. ***See Matthew 27:16, Mark 15:34, Luke 23:46, John 19:30.***

That is why holy spirit was described as being ***upon*** certain people in the Old Testament. Jesus had to fulfill the laws to be the Savior and then get up again in order for us to have that same power ***in* us by seed,** which is the new birth. By accurate definition, "born again" is not a religious phrase but an actual seed implantation and new birth by the spirit of God! Once in place, it cannot be removed; in contrast to spirit that was upon people in the Old Testament.

John 3:3-7
3 Jesus answered and said unto him, Verily, verily, I say unto thee, Except a man be born again, he cannot see the kingdom of God.
4 Nicodemus saith unto him, How can a man be born when he is old? Can he enter the second time into his mother's womb, and be born?
5 Jesus answered, Verily, verily, I say unto thee, Except a man be born of water and of the Spirit, he cannot enter into the kingdom of God.
6 That which is born of the flesh is flesh; and that which is born of the Spirit is spirit.
7 Marvel not that I said unto thee, Ye must be born again.

We are not going to get into a review of water and spiritual baptism here, we just want you to see that there is a new order with the fulfillment of Jesus and the law, and what is now available because of that.

> ***Ephesians 1:19 & 20***
> *And what is the exceeding greatness of his power to usward who believe, according to the working of his mighty power, Which he wrought in Christ, when he raised him from the dead, and set him at his own right hand in the heavenly places.*

Now back to the question of ***Does a person need to be born again (saved) before the person can be healed? No.*** For years, evangelists and healers have gone into nations that are Hindu, Muslim, Buddhist and all nationalities and wherever the Word has been taught, or people have been ministered to, God has healed them even when they did not believe in Jesus.

Many have been healed through the teaching of the Word. Once the healing takes place, it is a wake-up call; the unbeliever wants some of that! They see the power and this open door to salvation. Healings can be one of the best tools in evangelism. It has been proven that way in Africa, India, China and in many other nations. Glory to God!

> ***Psalms 107:20***
> *He sent his word, and healed them, and delivered them from their destructions.*

This New Birth is something very special. The Word says we are sealed up with the "*holy spirit of promise*" ***(Ephesians 1:13)***. Sealed means "canned up" in another text. We cannot lose it. This holy spirit you have been sealed with is the earnest; the down payment, of our inheritance until Christ returns! Glory Hallelujah!

We are told in ***I John 3:2*** *"Beloved,* ***now*** *are we the sons of God, and it doth not yet appear what we shall be: but we know that, when he shall appear, we shall be like him; for we shall see him as he is."* Well Amen and Amen! What does this mean in our daily life? Well, our prayers for others and for ourselves need not be hindered. We can approach God for anything, and literally, we have the same power of Christ in us that God used when He raised Christ from the dead!
It means that **Mark 16: 17-18** are true for us and

we can start using that power in helping others, as well! **17a** and ***18b***:

Mark 16: 17a, 18

17a And these signs shall follow them that believe: In my name shall they cast out devils...

18b They shall lay hands on the sick, and they shall recover.

We want to focus on these verses that will help prepare us to step into operating a ministry of healing and deliverance.

8 Ministry of Deliverance

Another facet of Jesus' ministry was a ministry of deliverance

The Ministry of deliverance deals with casting out spirits that many times oppress and possess individuals. Over 50% of Jesus's ministry was healing and casting out spirits. Spirits can cause many malfunctions and diseases in a person. Many times when the spiritual influence is cast out, the body heals itself naturally, the way God designed it.

We will look at a couple of instances when Jesus confronted people that were possessed with spirits. Another word for possessed would be demonized. In Mark there is an example of one of the most radical possessions of a person that you will find in the Word of God.

Mark 5: 1-17

1 And they came over unto the other side of the sea, into the country of the Gadarenes.

2 And when he was come out of the ship, immediately there met him out of the tombs, a man with an unclean spirit,

3 Who had his dwelling among the tombs; and no man could bind him, no, not with chains:

4 Because that he had been often bound with fetters and chains, and the chains had been plucked asunder by him, and the fetters broken in pieces: neither could any man tame him.

5 And always, night and day, he was in the mountains, and in the tombs, crying, and cutting himself with stones.

6 But when he saw Jesus afar off, he ran and worshiped him,

7 And cried with a loud voice, and said, What have I to do with thee, Jesus, thou Son of the most high God? I adjure thee by God, that thou torment me not.

8 For he said unto him, Come out of the
man, thou unclean spirit.
9 And he asked him, What is thy name?
And he answered, saying, My name is
Legion: for we are many.
10 And he besought him much that he
would not send them away out of the
country.
11 Now there was nigh unto the mountains
a great herd of swine feeding.
12 And all the devils besought him, saying,
Send us into the swine, that we may enter
into them.
13 And forthwith Jesus gave them leave.
And the unclean spirits went out, and
entered into the swine: and the herd ran
violently down a steep place into the sea.
14 And they that fed the swine fled, and
told it in the city, and in the country. And
they went out to see what it was that was
done.
15 And they come to Jesus, and see him
that was possessed with the devil, and had
the legion, sitting, and clothed, and in his
right mind: and they were afraid.

It is hard to imagine this man being so possessed

that he would have a legion. In the first century, a legion could be as many as 6000 soldiers. What a deliverance this had to be! This man was completely delivered as we can see in verse 18.

> ***Mark 5:18***
> *And when he was come into the ship, he that had been possessed with the devil prayed him that he might be with him.*

The man wanted to hang out with Jesus out of gratitude. Can you imagine becoming the real person God wanted you to be after all of that?

Another account is in Matthew Chapter 9.

> ***Matthew 9:31-35***
> *31 But they, when they were departed, spread abroad his fame in all that country.*
> *32 As they went out, behold, they brought to him a dumb man possessed with a devil.*
> *33 And when the devil was cast out the dumb spake: and the multitudes marveled, saying, It was never so seen in Israel.*
> *34 But the Pharisees said, He casteth out devils through the prince of the devils.*
> *35 And Jesus went about all the cities and*

villages, teaching in their synagogues, and preaching the gospel of the kingdom, and healing every sickness and every disease among the people.

Isn't that great?! Once that dumb spirit was removed, the man could talk. Hallelujah! Of course the Pharisees accused him of casting out devils by the prince of devils.

I remember hearing a minister at one time saying "People want to criticize things that they cannot produce". The thing is, if they only knew and believed, they could produce these miracles themselves!

John 14:12
Verily, verily, I say unto you, He that believeth on me, the works that I do shall he do also; and greater works than these shall he do; because I go unto my Father.

There is no time limit on what Jesus was able to do; the only instruction was *believe on me*. When Jesus sent forth the 12 disciples in Matthew 10:5–8, verse 8 says, *"Heal the sick, cleanse the lepers, raise the dead, cast out devils: freely ye have*

received, freely give." The message for today is still the same.
A born-again believer with the spirit of Christ in him is capable to perform what Jesus did and, even greater works!

•

We were in a meeting in Orlando, with Rev. Wayne Clapp and Rev. Kevin Guigou. When the meeting ended a woman stood up and wanted 5-10 minutes of testimony time. Linda told her story about deliverance and how there is no shame to have this spiritual deliverance done in your life. Jesus didn't condemn anyone for having a spirit, whether it was possession, or just a spirit hanging around a person.

She indicated that at a prior time, Rev. Wayne Clapp had ministered to her. During this ministering, he asked God to send down a garbage truck and asked her what she saw in her mind. She said she saw a truck and six red dots. Wayne indicated those red dots were devil spirits and he was going to take them out. He started naming them and as he named them, he cast them into the dump truck. As she visualized them, she saw them moving into the truck.

It came down to the sixth one and he asked her what it looked like in her mind and all that she could see was just one red dot left jumping around wildly in her mind. This last spirit was bondage and it was commanded to be cast into the truck, then they visualized it being moved into the ocean as commanded by Wayne.

That bondage spirit was something that had kept her bound for almost 20 years over a divorce she had thought was all her fault. That spirit had kept her in bondage for all those years. The heaviness and all the guilt and everything else was completely removed from her. So many times people say when they are delivered, it is like they are floating, the heaviness is gone and there is just a lightness and joy and rejoicing that returns to them. Linda wanted to emphasize we have not because we ask not, so ask for help and don't wait!

•

The first time we started this type of deliverance ministering ourselves was about 8-9 years ago. There is a gentleman who lived in Orlando, who also was at the teaching meeting where Linda gave her testimony, Don C., who called about a week after the Orlando meeting to meet Judi and me. He came over on a Friday, spent all day and discussed everything except his spiritual needs and then he returned to Orlando, still in torment and agitated.

The next day, he called early and said "I need to see you, again". I said we had other plans, and it just would not be a good time but he persisted in saying that he needed to see us. God put it on my spirit that it was a spiritual thing and so he made the two-hour trip.

During the trip, the devil tried to talk him out of coming; that he would be tired afterward, he would have to spend time there, lay down and take a nap and also Don said later that he had urges to turn around and return to Orlando.

We had been preparing and had read several books on deliverance ministry and had ideas on how to help him.

Once he arrived at the house, he told us that he was unable to, as a contractor, get his billings out. He had one invoice that was $20,000 and it had to be itemized and given to a woman (client), but once he did that, it would be paid immediately but he was just unable to do that. We had determined that, that was a spirit of procrastination.

In talking with him, he said that when he was 12 years old, his mother had cancer, she had been in the hospital, was returning this particular day. He had seven-year-old twin brothers that the Mother had asked, that while she was resting in bed, to keep them quiet. Well, the kids ran wild, slammed the door, his dad came home and scolded Don for not controlling his brothers.

That night, his mother died and for all these years; he was almost 30 years old when he came to us, he had a problem with guilt thinking that he caused his mother's demise. We had a piece of paper and wrote down GUILT. You didn't have to be a brain surgeon to know that that was a particular spirit that was tormenting him.

As we talked to him, we wrote down several other spirits that again, we felt were tormenting him. Judi and Don sat on the couch. Judi had her arm around him and I got in front of him and as we started ministering, God would give us a Word of

Knowledge. We had information that was specific to this situation that we could not have known because he had never told us anything about it.

One of the spirits we realized he had was a spirit of lying. Don was not lying but that spirit was lying to him, condemning him of many things in his life. We know that the devil is the great accuser but we have an advocate, we have a defense attorney and that advocate is Jesus, the son of God.

As we engaged; we got permission from Don to remove any spirits. We had said we would move that lying spirit off to the side and go in-depth into other things first. Well, we took out the spirit of guilt, because of that thing with his mother, then we moved onto some other spirits.

We were in amazement! This was the first time we had been doing that type of ministering and it was kind of a shock to us, yet it wasn't a shock that finally, **the spirit said in Don's voice** "These people don't know what they're doing". At that point, that really ticked me off so I called out that spirit of lying; we had to get rid of that lying spirit so we could move on to some others. While we were ministering to him, Don had his hands firmly pressed over his ears to not hear. This was a spirit controlling him.

One of the things that came up, was Filth. At the time, we did not know how that fit in yet, but we recognized that one. Having the correct name of a spirit is not always important, the deliverance of the one being attacked is important. Though we might not have the correct name of the spirit, it still has to leave because the name we need to know is Jesus, "*which is above every name*," (***Philippians 2:9***.)

One other thing I had written down was the spirit of slumber and this spirit is not anything that necessarily has anything to do with sleeping, but it is a spirit that appears to make something look like it is not, or, it obscures something. For example, if you pull up to a stop sign and a car is bearing down on you, you look right at it but don't see it, pull right out in front of it and BAM, you get hit!

I knew that it was something like "slumber" but I didn't know what to call it, so I put it off to the side of the list and towards the end of the session Judi said "I feel he has the spirit of slumber" and Mike said "Oh, yes, yes, that's it. Cast that spirit out." That is what we were doing; as God put it on our hearts through the whole thing, we kept casting out the different spirits.

Don was completely delivered. He was able to have lightness; the heaviness that we talked about, left him. He said he felt like he was floating on air. He wanted to eat. He did not have to take a nap, it was just a joyful moment and we just gave the Father and His son, Jesus, the praise and the glory.

The next day when he was home, he got all of his billing caught up and the client who had the $20,000 invoice, paid him immediately upon receipt of it. The filthiness had to do with all the pop cans and trash in his truck which he cleaned out. It was just a joyful time to see how the heart of God is that we have complete deliverance, that we can have peace that passes all understanding. We also encourage you to step forward in a meeting to receive your healing, or go to those around you, don't wait for a special occasion.

Mike: We were in a Jesus healing and deliverance teaching Greensboro, NC. Several people taught that day, including Judi and I, to a small group of about 70 people. After the teaching, there was gentleman about 50 years of age who was unknown to us, approached us, walking and with a slight tremor in his hands. We asked him what he came for and he said "I came for my deliverance from Parkinson's disease" which he had been fighting for about twelve years.

We started ministering to him, he was then shaking heavily; the spirit that was controlling the situation was not excited about losing its happy home. I asked for those believers around us to start speaking in tongues out loud; for spirits do not like this power of God.

The shaking was almost getting out of control so we knew that we needed some support. We asked Pastor Tonia Shroyer to come and get involved; she is particularly strong at deliverance ministry. Tonia asked the man to look directly into her eyes; there is an expression about the eyes being the window to the soul and many times you can see the spirits in the eyes of a person. Sometimes, one of the pupils will be constricted.

The man was shaking so badly that he could barely stand. His upper body seemed to be fine but his legs were like rubber flopping around. God told

Tonia by Word of Knowledge to have him walk. I'm thinking *this guy can't even stand!*
Tonia got on one side of the man and I got on the other to give him support until he starting moving his legs. I'm thinking *Jesus, we've got all these people here, don't let us down, don't let us look foolish!* This was just my old man; unbelief, on my part.

As we started walking him around this big room, he said "I want to run!" I'm thinking *holy moly!* but the man started to run, God put on my heart to set up a "fire tunnel." I had only seen this one other time in my life but we lined up two rows of people across from each other, with hands touching in the middle. As he ran through the "tunnel" I told the people to prophesy over him, give him a touch or say encouraging words as he passed through. He liked it so much that he wanted to run through again and by this time, he was running all around the inside of the room. We found out later that he used to be a runner but had lost all hope of ever being able to do that again.

WOW! God sure is good! I always think of something Pastor Billy Burke told us several years ago: *Never lose your WOW Factor.* Every time

God does something like this, you just have to stand up and shout out *WOW!*

After the service where many people were healed, there was entertainment and I watched this same man as he sat calmly, not shaking, through the whole two hours. He walked out healed and delivered. Even if the trip had been just for him, it would have been worth it. As the Word says, "*He* (Jesus) *is able to save them to the uttermost that come unto God by him, seeing he ever liveth to make intercession for them.*" ***(Hebrews 7:25.)***

You can never be down too far that he cannot pick you up by your bootstraps. It was all accomplished on the cross, on a hill at Calvary over 2000 years ago. Glory Hallelujah!!!

We also want to share with you the power we have in Christ in breaking off generational or inherited conditions or "curses" of diseases and sickness. Many things we attribute as solely a physical condition, is actually spiritually-based and can be passed through the generations. You can read the gospel accounts of some in Mark 1:26, 9:18, 20, 39 & 42.

The first time in the Word that a generational curse is talked about is in ***Deuteronomy 5:9b***... *"visiting the iniquity of the fathers upon the children unto the third and fourth generation of them that hate me."*

However, in Galatians, the Word declares that we can be freed from curses.

> ***Galatians 3:13***
> *Christ has redeemed us from the curse of the law, being made a curse for us: for it is written Cursed is every one that hangeth on a tree.*

That curse was about three things:
1.) No one was able to fulfill the law.
2.) There was no way of being guaranteed eternal life.
3.) People lived in the diseases under the sin of not following the law which had ruler-ship over a person, which led to people not receiving their healing and fear of death. However, in Galatians 4:4-6 we are told:

> ***Galatians 4:4-6***
> 4 *But when the fullness of the time was*

come, God sent forth his Son, made under the law
5 To redeem them that were under the law, that we might receive the adoption (son-ship) of sons.
6 And because ye are sons, God hath sent for the Spirit of his Son into your hearts, crying, Abba, Father.

Our biggest weaponry is ***speaking the truth***, especially ***to*** the circumstance or condition. Jesus spoke to the fig tree (Matthew 21:19, Mark 11:14) itself. Since the Word tells me I can break off that heart disease that my great-grandfather and my father had, I'm going to break that spirit of inheritance and make a decree that the disease stops and goes no further. We do not say, "*The disease runs in my family so I will probably get it.*" No, No, No!

Psalms 107:2
Let the redeemed of the Lord say so, whom he hath redeemed from the hand of the enemy.

If you are fighting a health situation, praying and waiting until your healing comes, then say "I'm fighting this situation", not, "I have this condition the doctors said was terminal".

Notice also that when Jesus spoke to the fig tree, he did it with authority and ***commanded*** it in the imperative mood. We too, need to declare things with the authority and power of Christ or the results will be lacking if not present at all. We do not beg, but command healing in the name of Jesus!

Keys: Binding spirits and where they go is seen in the gospels with Jesus in Matthew 12:43-45:

> ***Matthew 12:43-45***
> *43 When the unclean spirit is gone out of a*
> *man, he walketh through dry places,*
> *seeking rest and findeth none.*
> *44 Then he saith, I will return into my*
> *house*
> *from whence I came out; and when he is*
> *come, he findeth it empty, swept, and*
> *garnished,*
> *45 Then goeth he, and taketh with himself*
> *seven other spirits more wicked than*
> *himself, and they enter in and dwell there:*
> *and the last state of that man is worse than*

the first. Even so shall it be also unto this wicked generation.

This passage has some important points to consider. It is significant that we are told there are spirits and how they operate. We are told what to do to keep ourselves from getting in a worse situation than when we started. We are to guard our minds and if we do not renew our minds to the Word, it is possible even more spirits come back; and they usually don't travel alone. This record also tells us there are degrees or levels of wickedness in the spirit kingdom. See also Luke 11:24-26.

Our power base is using that name of Jesus where "*every knee has to bow,*" (***Philippians 2:*10)** and commanding with authority what needs to happen. When we are in deliverance ministry, we want to deactivate those spirits; bind them up and send them to that dry place where they can do no harm. See Matthew 16:19 and Matthew 18:18.

Matthew 18:18
Verily I say unto you, Whatsoever ye shall bid on earth shall be bound in heaven: and whatsoever ye shall loose on earth

shall be loosed in heaven.

Other people walking in the power of God...

A healing of Mary and Matt *(pseudonyms)* ***as told by Mark and Juany H. in a letter to the Magels about Mary, the mother of her adult son, Matt:***

We have to tell you about our first intense experience in a Deliverance situation. Mark reached out to a man in his same profession and they conversed about a medical condition that Matt has that he seeks treatment from here in the Tampa area. On his last day here, he came to see us to take us up on the offer of laying on of hands, receiving a ministering of healing, that Mark offered. After some rescheduling, the man and his mother came to our apartment.

They came and started talking about their many illnesses and afflictions. We talked The Word for a little while; these are people that minister to others, they know The Word and the name of Jesus. Then we started ministering to the mom, commanding the spirit of fear to come out and all of a sudden, she started twitching and moving weirdly and started saying “No, no, no! I don’t want to leave”!

I told her “Mary, look at me in the eyes!” and Mark and I were commanding that sucker to come out and, telling Mary to cast it out herself, as well. Then we commanded the spirit of hatred; and oh man, Mary looked at me and grunted, made animalistic faces and gnashed her teeth. Same thing; we commanded it out and Ruby did as well. We cast out other spirits and she seemed to be fine, so we moved on to the son.

God gave both of us a Word of Knowledge in things Matt had not even expressed. He made some noises but we cast them out. Mark and I went back and forth and Matt commanded them (concerning) himself.

Mary started making some weird moves and I asked if she was OK and another spirit manifested itself. It didn’t want to leave and I asked “Mary, do you know about speaking in tongues?” She did and I instructed her to speak in tongues out loud. She said she had been under the influence of controlling spirits but I did not fully understand; I thought we had already cast that one out.

We kept ministering to Matt because he kept bringing things up that he wanted to be ministered for. He had a broken finger and a little cast around his thumb. I felt inspired to ask Mary to minister to him and she came and was so bold! Matt took the cast off the finger, touched it, bent his thumb and he had no more pain. His thumb had been restored, right in front of our eyes!

After that, we were chatting like old time friends. Mary was so changed. When she first arrived, she looked old and scared; and now she was all chatty and free. I love seeing that deliverance in people's lives. Matt told Mark "Dude, I had no idea you were such a freak for Jesus like me!"

Two days later, it was on Mark's heart that we should call Mary and when she returned my call, she said that she was having suicidal thoughts and was addicted to nicotine supplements and could not sleep.

When she came by our apartment the next morning, we started talking a little and then she started twitching again. She was snarling and she said "This is not me making these movements.

Mark and I both commanded the spirit of suicide to go and it started saying *"She's mine! Leave her alone!"* We told it that was a lie, that Mary belongs to the Most High God. The spirit said that she had pills at home and it would make her take those pills. We kept ministering; suggested to her to get rid of the sleeping pills, she was healed now and she could give it a try to sleep on her own.

Then we cast out addiction to the nicotine supplements and it started saying "*But where am I going to go? I help her.*" We said that wasn't our problem, it had to leave now. Mary then said that she has been under the affliction of controlling spirits; not herself, but others around her have afflicted her. That one did not want to go when I told it to go; it fought it. I said it would go to the bottomless pit. I reminded it of its future; the lake of fire!

Man! When I said that, Mary started screaming out loud for about ten seconds at the top of her lungs. We wondered what the neighbors were thinking but God must have sound-proofed the room! After that, Mary said that she was so tired that she needed to rest.

We gave her some material from the Word, *The Encourager* magazine and teaching CDs from Christian Family Fellowship so she could fill up her mind with the Word. Previously, we had given her and her son *How To Heal The Sick* from Frances and Charles Hunter. We gave her some practical advice on some things; a great way to retain healing is to give a testimony about her own healing.

She texted me in the afternoon, saying that she was at a clinic and she did give her testimony to another lady, prayed for that woman, and that woman was delivered! In giving the details of this healing and deliverance episode, we do not want to magnify what the devil spirits do, it was just the first time that we lived the deliverance experience. The best part is that we were so energized, so ready to help. I feel God has begun to send us His beloved people that are heavily afflicted because he knows we can help them.

We are beginning to understand, in the *ginōskō*; the experiential way, the authority of the name of Jesus and the power of mentioning his blood! This all happened because Mark reached out to someone on-line that was a total stranger through the door of similar professional work.

•

After spirits have gone to a dry place, they stay for a period of time. In this time, people need to continually study and fortify themselves with The Word of God, praise God and Jesus for their deliverance, tell other people, and engage in helping minister to others to get their healing or deliverance so the spirits are unable to return. Testimonies are so big in the lives of Christians!

9 Testimonies

Key: Giving testimony is a very important part of a person's deliverance.

> ***Revelation 12:11***
> *And they overcame him by the blood of the lamb and by the word of their testimony and they loved not their lives unto death.*

Whenever we receive a healing or deliverance, we do need to testify and give God the Father, and His son, Jesus, the glory, praise Him and go in thankfulness. In the later part of Jeremiah Chapter 17, vs 26 it says that we are to bring sacrifices of praise unto the Lord.

> ***Jeremiah 33:11***

The voice of joy, the voice of gladness, the voice of the bridegroom, the voice of the bride, the voice of them that shall say Praise the Lord of Hosts for the Lord is good for his mercy endureth forever. And of them that shall bring the sacrifice of praise into the house of the Lord for I will cause a return of captivity of the land as the first sayeth the Lord.

Psalm 100:4
Enter into his gates with thanksgiving, and into his courts with praise: be thankful unto him, and bless his name.

The two key words are praise and thankfulness.

I used to think that discussing testimonies about the healing and deliverance that we had ministered to was like bragging, yet I found in the Word that when the disciples came back from their mission, they 'rehearsed' what was done in the name of Jesus. **See Acts 14:27.**

The Word asks "What is the worth of a soul?" Well Jesus thought you were worth dying for. Whatever the price something is worth is whatever you can sell it for. Well Jesus became a propitiation for us by lying down his life. We have that forgiveness and remission of sins and so do others, if they only knew it!

Every chance we get, we stop and talk to strangers, we do these things that might appear odd or even outlandish; the growing out of the legs and arms such because we want to reach as many people as we can!

"By his stripes," it says in Peter, that "*we WERE healed.*" ***(I Peter 2:24.)*** Christ already made the payment but if that is kept a secret, then people won't walk in health or salvation. Get it?

Jesus wants His church, the body, to be without spot, without wrinkle and without blemish. In these last days, it talks about pouring out his spirit upon all flesh. We are definitely seeing more and more revival in this country even though the country has, in so many areas, become so wicked and perverse.

•

We need to give God praise. The horn, the trumpet

and the shofar in the Old Testament were used for many reasons. We ran into a woman who had a testimony. Five guys who stood around her with shofars, blew them and she was healed of stage four cancer. They blew the shofars and she was healed! Now that's radical! We could have said "Now we don't do that in our church, that's not right", but we have to get radical. All through the Bible, God has been radical!

Pastor Phil Derstine of Christian Retreat said once "The kids need to be radical, in a good way. Otherwise, they will grow up to be like their parents." We want to be bold! Try to get out of the habit of thinking that God will or will not do something a certain way; just get out of the way and let Him work.

Naaman had to go out and dip 7 times in the Jordan; why was he healed on the 7th time and not on the first time? We have seen this with repeating Holy Communion several days in a row, and on the last day, the person is healed. This was the instruction at times so that is what we told the person, they did it, and got their healing.

Jesus Christ and the record of mud and sticking it

on guys' eyes. God has been radical! Talking donkeys, groups of angels that only one person could see! We need to shake up the *inside* of the church sometime and get a little radical ourselves!

> ***Acts 19:11***
> *And God wrought special miracles by the hands of Paul so that from his body were brought unto the sick handkerchiefs or aprons, and the diseases departed from them, and the evil spirits went out of them.*

We do not need to explain everything that God does or know why He does what He does. Just be humble enough to do what God tells you to do.

Psalms 62:19 declares, "*They shall bring forth fruit in old age.*" They shall be full of sap, verve, trust, love and contentment. We should be living memorials to show that God is upright and faithful to His promise. First thing you know, they'll bronze us!

•

Mike: Our little four year old granddaughter, Ashleigh, and her sister, Mallery, were down in

Florida. They decided they wanted to go with Paw-Paw to get pizza. When we came back, Ashleigh got out of the car and slammed the car door on her hand and crushed it! I could hear the screaming. I ran around the car and saw it. It looked terrible. Mallery was just standing there looking at it and I said "Open the door!" and we did and I said "Well right now, in the name of Jesus we are going to pray for it, it is going to be healed, the pain is going to be gone and God is going to heal you."

When I said those things, immediately, all the pain stopped. She just looked at it, shook her hand around. We went upstairs, she showed it to everybody. It looked terrible. The next day, after Ahleigh woke up, I asked her how her hand was. She put out both hands and looked at them and she couldn't tell which hand it was. It was perfect! No bruising or anything.

Praise the Lord! She said "God healed me". "You remember this day, you remember this day, don't ever forget it", I said, "because what God did for you this day, He will continue to do for the rest of your life! He will do that for you."

We went out for dinner one night with this couple

not long after that. The woman had her arm in a cast, she was talking about it and Ashleigh asked "Did God heal it?" The woman said "Yes, I prayed for it and everything" but Ashleigh said "Well God healed my hand" and Ashleigh gave her testimony. It brought tears to my eyes.

•

My grandson, Branden, was 14 when he went to teen camp (at Christian Family Fellowship, Tipp City, OH) the first time. Judi asked him when he came back home "What stuck out in your mind the most?" The first thing he said was "It was the testimonies. I really liked the testimonies!"

•

Jake's Testimony

I had injured my right shoulder in a motorcycle accident with a deer and came out with what a doctor diagnosed as a torn rotator cuff. It was excruciating! I was waiting for surgery to be scheduled but we went to Ohio and my wife insisted that we hook up with the Magels; I had heard about their ability with God to heal and on that morning, I was actually in tears, the shoulder hurt so badly. I couldn't even lift my arm above my waist.

Mike, Judi and Sue laid their hands on the shoulder and ministered to me and they said afterwards that they could feel movement in the shoulder when they prayed but I didn't feel anything. I believed God could heal me but had to ask myself, *Why would He heal me?* I wanted to be healed, though. Afterward, when Mike asked me to do something I could not do before, I immediately raised that arm up above my head! I did windmills around and around with it!

My thoughts on it? My viewpoint on it is: AIN'T GOD GREAT??!!! I tell everybody about that!

Note from Judi: Jake had so much movement, I thought he was putting us on; that he was moving the wrong shoulder as a joke!....There was another man there with shoulder pain so we had Jake minister healing to him. It is good to have the one healed turn around and minister to someone else. It builds confidence in the power of God...the power of testimonies in action.

God At The Garage Sale

Mike: Not too long ago we went together with our children and had a garage sale in their neighborhood. A lady came to the garage sale, she bought several things and as she was writing a check I noticed her fingers were going sideways, I mean going sideways and she's trying to write this check!

I said "*Hey, God's in the business of healing those hands, (*Emphatically) *God's in the business of healing those hands!"* She said I pray every day and everything. Well, she had a meeting she had to go to, so she went and came back to exchange cash for the check and we took her into the house and talked to her about her fingers and what God wants for her.

We said "*We're going to minister to you in the name of Jesus Christ,we are going to talk to those fingers in the name of Jesus*!" and so we did, and my gosh! The movement in her hands and her arms wrists were immediately changed, but her fingers were not completely straightened out so we told her "Well, you know what, you keep praying for them in the morning, you just keep rubbing them and thanking God to straighten them out completely." I mean she's going, "*Glory be to God, Hallelujah! Hallelujah!*" That's the way it oughta be, that's the way it oughta be. She told us, she said, "*This is the best garage sale I've ever been to!* **Why? Because God was in the garage sale!"** We always put out some the teaching CDs we have already heard. One woman showed up and told us "*I don't even know why I came here but now I do*"; she got a bunch of those CDs and sent them to South America. Praise the Lord!

Robbing patients from the doctor

Mike: We go to the doctors' offices quite often; not necessarily for us, but for Judi's Mom and while they're doing something, getting a shot or something, I'm out there ministering to people in the doctor's office.

We had one guy, he had a growth behind his ear; they were from VanWert, Ohio, and I just started talking to him and said "What are you in here for?" The man showed me and said he had a growth and I said "Well God can take care of that, God can heal that, so why don't I pray for you…I was by myself on that one, so I prayed for him and then all this stuff just started running out of that cyst or whatever that thing was. It was like it had been lanced. I believe the guy was healed, I gave him a card, let him know where I was located. I believe God is in and behind these things that we are seeing and doing.

> ***Philippians 2:13***
> *For it is God which worketh in you both to will and to do of his good pleasure.*

Mike and the lady at Wendy's

Mike: Hey there was one Wednesday, I was at home, I was studying the Word, I was jumping around like a dag-gone jack rabbit or something. I've got books around here and books around there and I see something in the Word and I'm excited!
I decided Wendy's sounds good for lunch. I'll get me some chili and a baked potato and I only have to go down the street here and so I get in the car and I hear this little voice say, "*Go to the one in Troy.*" Well, this one is shorter but I turn around and OK, I'll go to the one in Troy. Didn't even think about it.

I'm sitting in the one in Troy eating, about finished my meal, and this woman gets up with a walker.

She didn't have far to go to get outside, course I'm trying to eat my meal so I can get going and I see her getting in the car and I run out there and I'm thinking, "*Walker, bad leg,*" wouldn't you think that?

I asked her, "*So what's the matter with that leg*?" She says, "*It's not the leg, its leukemia.*" I said "*You know what lady*?", I said, "*I'm a minister*" (like I say, this opens the door) "*...and I was going to this Wendy's in Tipp City and God told me to come here and what do you suppose, Darlene*"; her name is Darlene, "*God sent me here for? For you! God sent me here for you! He did not send me here to blow smoke.*"

"*I mean I am expecting, you should expect, that when I pray for you, that you are going to get healed. God didn't just bring me here for nothin'*!", so I ministered to her, I gave her my card, she and her husband lived down in Dayton, I don't know but I expect to hear from them that she is healed. I don't believe God would send me there unless there was a purpose. Our lives have a purpose and us old people, we have a purpose.

Judi: Everybody has situations. You don't live in

this world for very long and not have attacks, and it just comes with the territory and the harvest is great. How great do you want that Holy Spirit in you to be? It's up to you to digest the Word, to believe it and walk out on it.

Judi with Gail in Montana

We ministered to several of the people in the home-based fellowship there. They have old-old, middle-aged, teens and youngsters; we all have needs and situations. Gail, our hostess, thought the people were tired and wanted everyone else to be taken of, but Gail had a need. She said she had this pain in her back, whenever she touched it, it was painful. Her hips are un-level; one leg shorter, so Mike sat her down. She'd lived with this pain for 12 years and had become so accustomed to it, she forgot about it until Mike brought it up first. We saw that when Mike sat her in a chair, one leg was about 2 inches shorter than the other. She also had a cough after having breathed in chlorine from her swimming pool and she wanted that ministered to, also. They started with the cough and then Mike said "Is there something wrong with your back?" (Gail had fallen at a roller rink twelve years before.)

God grew the one leg out, ministered to her, then she had no pain. Immediately after ministering you want to get them to do something they could not do before, and to offer praise and thanks. By the way, nobody has to close their eyes during these things; everyone should see the miracles happening right before their eyes!

When we asked one man; a big rough-necked fighting kind of man what he wanted, he said "*I'm mad, I'm fat, I'm diabetic*"! We ministered to him and took the spirit of anger and hate out of him in the name of Jesus.

God doesn't care the words you use, you just say it, the man knew within himself he didn't want to be like this and what was wrong and he didn't want to be that way, he wanted to be different. He was humble and meek and very emotional. We did this one privately in another room. He said afterwards that he believed we were sent there just for him.

Sometimes, you may need to ask family members to leave the room. (Mark 5:39-42) God will let you know if something needs to be handled privately and getting other people out may be because of their unbelief.

Again, we want to repeat that there is no shame attached to finding out there are spirits that have been affecting or operating in your own life and if you are just now learning about this, or even have seen and know this, just go get the help you need to be your best for God. Go to a spirit-filled church or person that knows about spiritual warfare and delivered.

Regarding how to figure out what God is leading you to do with spirits, the great healing team (now deceased) of Charles and Frances Hunter's said in their classes "When in doubt, cast it out, or grow it out". We don't care what's there, we just want it out! We know we have an enemy so if he can talk us out of something, or whatever lie it is he is telling you, he'll use it against you so that you will not get your deliverance.

Especially at a time of healing and deliverance, the lies will come out. The devil is the father of lies, he cannot, will not, tell the truth. He can counterfeit healing but he can't actually do it. A house divided against itself; if the devil did healing, his house would collapse. See Chapter

12: The Devil Doesn't Heal.

Mark 3:25 & 26 in the Amplified
And if a house is divided (split into factions and rebelling against itself, that house will not be able to last. And if satan has raised an insurrection against himself and is divided, he cannot stand but is (surely) coming to an end.

See also Luke 11:17-18. Especially when we receive a healing or deliverance, we do need to testify and give God the Father, and his son, Jesus, the glory, praise Him and go in thankfulness.

> ***I Peter 4:11***
> *If any man speak, let him speak as the oracles of God; if any man minister, let him do it as of the ability which God giveth: that God in all things may be glorified through Jesus Christ, to whom be praise and dominion for ever and ever. Amen.*

There are four things I would instruct a person who just received their healing and want to keep it, to do.

1.) Immediately give praise and thanks to Jesus and to the Father. Continue to praise them, much.

2.) Be thankful. Give thanks about all the wonderful things you have in your life, things in God's Word (Philippians 4:8) and continue to stay thankful.

3.) Give your testimony. Tell people what God has done for you.

4.) Fill your head with the Word.

Check out the promises God has given us, memorize powerful scripture, make the Word yours. If you need healing, memorize those promises about health. You are prepared then to come against attacks with the truth. See Chapter 13, Healing Scriptures.

In Hosea 4:6a, God tells us why His people are destroyed: "*My people are destroyed for lack of knowledge,*" and it is not a lack of knowledge of the world. It is because we lack a knowledge of the truth of the Word, or fail to believe it is the truth and we don't believe the integrity of the Word.

In the Amplified version, I John 3:8 tells us "*The reason the son of God was made manifest* (visible) *was to undo (destroy, loosen and dissolve) the* *works the devil (has done).”* This establishes John 10:10 that there are two distinct forces at work in the world, one that works for good, and one that works for evil. We choose who we are going to believe and activate results by what we say, ourselves.

> ***Proverbs 18:20 & 21***
> *A man's belly shall be satisfied with the fruit of his mouth; and with the increase of his lips shall he be filled. Death and life are in the power of the tongue: and they that love it shall eat the fruit thereof.*

In the later part of Jeremiah Chapter 17, verse 26 it says that we are to bring sacrifices of praise unto the Lord.

> ***Jeremiah 33:11***
> *The voice of joy , the voice of gladness, the voice of the bridegroom, the voice of the bride, the voice of them that shall say Praise the Lord of Hosts for the Lord is good for his mercy endureth forever. And of them that shall bring the sacrifice of praise into the house of the Lord for I will cause a return of captivity of the land as*

the first sayeth the Lord.

In direct contrast to what we know the devil has for us, we need to remember the converse, is also true of our Lord.

> ***John 10:10 Amplified Version***
> *The thief comes only in order to steal and kill and destroy. I came that they may have and enjoy life, and have it in abundance (to the full, till it overflows).*

The Word asks "What is the worth of a soul?" Well Jesus though you were worth dying for. Whatever the price something is worth, is whatever you can sell it for. Jesus became a propitiation for us by laying down his life. We have that forgiveness and remission of sins. Our thanks and praise should be always pouring out in return for the life Christ made available to us!

Mike and Judi out of the box with Dr. Jesus

Our life has gotten so busy. We have gotten people coming out of the woodwork that we ministered to years ago. We had a woman who called and said "*I know you minister healing and I have this bad hip that goes out so I wondered, could I come over there*?" She came over and we ministered to her and I believe she received her healing, though I haven't talked to her in awhile.

Then she brought out a picture of her daughter. She (the woman) is from Malaysia, her husband is from the UK and the daughter is going to some fancy school out in Pennsylvania, in one of those expensive private schools. It was about finals time and the daughter had depression and stuff; just down and out. We said "*Well we can get her on the phone, pray for her over the phone; it* (ministering) *works over the phone*" but she said "*Oh no, I don't think so*," like that, "*But I have this picture*," so I said "OK*, put the picture down*".

We all three put our hands on it; we ministered to the picture. So it was a day or two later, the mother called and said "*It all lifted*!" Praise the Lord. You just can't say how God or Dr. Jesus are going to do their work.

•

Judi: Working with other people in this day and time is just a joy. We learn how to work with different people; what their strengths are, when to lead, when to stay quiet, what is needed in a given situation. Reverend Tonia can see the long-suits; the gold in people, what people are really suited to do. She is such an encourager, she really brings out the gold. "Give me a word of encouragement" she says to God, she puts them in the spot to where their ministry can grow and flourish. We are blessed to be a blessing. That's what goes through her mind, as Tonia gives out, she is blessing others and that is what God wants us to do as lights of the world.

We feel extremely honored and privileged that Reverend Tonia allows us the freedom to travel with her to various locations and meet so many folks with her. What joy it is to see God working with her and blessing the body of Christ!

> ***Genesis 12:2***
> *and I will make of thee a great nation, and*
> *I will bless thee, and make thy name great;*
> *and though shalt be a blessing.*

Working in teams

We love to work with Rev. Tonia Shroyer. She'll do an interview and get to the root of the problem.

She gets a lot of revelation, she talks about "Painting with Jesus"; her revelations. It's like going to the movies because she'll get revelation or a vision (it's different for every person) for that situation.

She spoke to a woman and said she saw an old-time switchboard with an operator plugging in wires. The wires were all lit up but the family members' lines had been disconnected so it was her job to plug them back in… The woman being ministered to, would be the one to do the reconnecting. Tonia will take the vision part herself, then she asks us to minister healing to various parts of the body. We may all three get the same information about the person being ministered to… Tears are coming down all of our faces.

Rev. Tonia Shroyer ran into a man, Joe D., at a chiropractor's office. There was one seat left and he sat down by her. They started talking, he asked what she did, she replied that she was a minister, he said "Oh, a minister…! He was thrilled. He has a huge compassionate heart, wants to evangelize, wants to get people born again and make sure everyone gets to heaven.

He suggested meeting his minister and do ministering-praying for people in his church. Tonia called us and we met at a restaurant. Joe brought his minister along. Afterward, we used the shaded church steps next door to the parking lot *(I told you that Billy Burke prophesied over us that our ministry would happen a lot in parking lots, didn't I?),* another couple came with them, and the man with Parkinson's was very moved after we ministered to him.

We learned he was not of Pastor Lynn's church but Tonia went to Romans 10:9 & 10 and explained the New Birth. We learned later that the man kept showing improvement and started attending Pastor Lynn and Joe's church. Joe is a farmer who rides a tractor and had a bad back. We had him sit on those church steps, grew out his legs and he had an arm and a shoulder that was healed, also.

Judi: Then we went over to Joe's farm and ministered to the hired man there. We grew out his leg in the kitchen. His ankles were completely off; not aligned. He told that hired man, "Now keep your eyes open and you can see God go to work, watch your miracle happen." They all saw the adjustment take place with their eyes. He instantly got relief from the pain in his back. He asked if they were going to church and he said yes.

Since then, Joe, who wants to know more about healing, said that he is taking a sabbatical, so that Mike and Judi can teach him (Joe). He'd wanted to speak in tongues for 15 years and so we and Rev. Kevin Guigou led him into speaking in tongues. Joe was so excited! He wants everybody to go to heaven and wants everybody healed.

A family member of Joe D., Christine, received some devastating news after having gone to two or three doctors and finally, an orthopedic specialist. They were looking at the X-Ray and it was thought the woman may have had an implant but it was actually a type of sarcoma. She said *"After seeing the X-Ray, I left the office feeling I had a death sentence."*

I called my brother's wife to tell her the news and without having heard it yet, I got a call from my cousin, Joe D., saying he had a strong thought to call. After hearing the bad news, Joe said that I should go see the Magels. We all decided to meet at my sister's home and I would meet "The

Healers".

There were 17 days in between the time I got the news and the time my insurance was approved for the pending surgery to remove the cancer. After Mike and Judi prayed for "jaw-dropping news", I believe I was healed. During this time, I attended a teaching and healing service of internationally-known Angus Buchan.

It was very crowded, we waited in line to be ministered to and I was going to leave but Joe said "I did not come all this way for Angus not to lay his hands on you." He was determined and within minutes, with a crowd around him, Angus put his hands on me and said "The cancer stops tonight!" and like Mike and Judi, he moved my arms around in ways that I could not move them, before.

Finally, I had the MRI and I went in for the results. The surgeon came in with tears in his eyes, sat on the stool and told me the MRI was 'perfect', and that he needed a moment. I smiled and said "The report was jaw-dropping, right?" He said yes. He also said he had to prove it to himself and asked me to have both shoulders X-Rayed again. I did and they were perfect.

On Angus Buchan's card is a verse that I have read many times:

> ***Psalms 37:4***
> *Delight thyself also in the Lord; and he shall give the desires of thine heart.*

When we look at all the people that were touched by the initial contact of Joe D, this shows the ripple-effect of each person just reaching out the way they feel inspired to do. You just cannot know the impact that one event will have on others. There was Joe, his minister and his wife, his employee and his family, Joe's cousin and husband, the surgeon of the cousin, and so it goes.

Judi: It is so rewarding to hear those testimonies, when the people call. It encourages us to keep growing and learning ways to help folks get their healing. God loves variety.

Compassion for people is a big key in successful deliverance and healing ministry. Remember that Jesus always did the will of his father and he looked at people with what? Compassion. Do a word study on that some time. Some concordances define *compassion* as *to love, to have the bowels yearning, to be merciful, suffering with another, to spare.* This is a deep-seated desire to share God's goodness, mercy and eternal life with people. When we begin to walk out on the truths of the Word of God as we see in Mark 16:18b, it is life-changing, not just for the people around you, but for you!

> **Mark 16:18b**
> *They shall lay hands on the sick, and they shall recover.*

Mike: People, we have to see this bigger, Bigger, BIGGER in our lives! We HAVE not just the instruction to carry this out but the *commission,* the *command* in the absolute sense of "shall", to do it. There is no waiting for a future moment or a future opportunity, to act.

A question we frequently get is ***When do I start ministering?*** *Is the bulk of the information you receive from God after you start to work, after you start praying, or before?*

Mike: With me, the specifics are *as I reach out or I am in prayer* so those folks who say we have to have permission from God to minister are languishing and not acting. If at the Bema (our place of rewards with Christ), we are shown a movie of the times we COULD have healed, but did not, what say you then? There is no magic formula to this, it is simply acting on a thought.

Well, what if it doesn't work? What if it does? You don’t take credit if it does work, and you don't take blame if it doesn't work. We don’t have a lot to do with it, we are just ministers for God and He gets the glory.

•

Charles and Frances Hunter, in their book *How Heal The Sick,* talk about how many hundreds of people they prayed for that did not appear to be immediately healed, but that did not keep them from going on and learning more with God.

You will notice also, in Jesus' healing ministry, there is not a long drawn-out prayer associated with the situation. He told us to do the healing by the laying on of hands. Can it be with oil or with the elders, with fasting? Can it be with prayer over a picture or through a cell phone? Is it one prayer, one time, or seven prayers or seven communions over seven days? Circling the city seven times or one time? We just do what God tells us and it is up to Him to do the work in getting it done. There are times that people seek us out and times that they have made fun of us for doing what we do.

Judi: In Florida (where we live part-time) there was a woman who made fun of us as we came in to the community room once, *There they are, those "healers"*, kind of mocking us, (sometimes we cannot do much in our own neighborhood because of their unbelief... (Matthew 13:58) But you know, it wasn't too long after that, that she called us up. She had some troubles, don't you know, and wanted our help. Well, we just laughed at her! No! Of course we didn't. We didn't bring up that other situation, we just helped her.

●

What about when we are in church? Shouldn't that be the place where things happen, not just be a social club? Pastor Billy Burke declared, *"If we go home from church and we are not healed and delivered, what good is the church?!...and if you are in a church where nobody is getting healed and they don't know what deliverance is, get out of there quick!"*

Mike: We are already in a place of people hearing. If people are standing up for ministering in church; they are already acknowledging they want to receive healing. All we have to do is to carry out what God puts on our heart with the person next to us!

> ***II Timothy 1:6-8***
> *6 Wherefore I put thee in remembrance that thou stir up the gift of God, which is in thee by the putting on of my hands*
> *7 For God hath not given us the spirit of fear; but of power, and of love, and of a sound mind.*
> *8 Be not thou therefore ashamed of the testimony of our Lord, nor of me his prisoner: but be thou partaker of the afflictions of the gospel according to the power of God.*

Are we going to live in expectation of the miraculous, the super-natural, the impossible? Life ***is*** the event you have been waiting for! The person you need to heal ***is*** the woman standing in front of you at the market, the mom at your school event who looks tired today or is at the store God told you to go to but you have no reason to go there. Instead of limiting God in your life and stating "Oh those things only happened to Paul or to Peter in those days of the early church", why not say continually, *Be it unto me according to thy will* and let God work the way He wills?

> ***Acts 5: 12-15***
> *12 And by the hands of* (insert your name!) *were many signs and wonders wrought among the people; (and they were all with one accord in Solomon's porch.*
> *13 And of the rest durst no man join himself to them: but the people magnified them.*
> *14 And believers were the more added to the Lord, multitudes both of men and women.)*
> *15 Insomuch that they brought forth the sick into the streets, and laid them on beds and couches, that at the least the shadow of Peter* (insert your name) *passing by might overshadow some of them.*

Remember too, that "*the gifts and calling of God are without repentance.*" ***(Romans 11:29)***

Romans 11:29 In the Amplified version:

For God's gifts and His call are irrevocable (He never withdraws them when once they are given, and, He does not change His mind about those to whom He gives His grace or to whom He sends His call).

We believe that as you read this book, if you are feeling encouraged, energized and excited about something that you know God has put on your heart to do; perhaps long ago, but never have, just thank Him for this precious assignment that He gave to you and take steps today, start learning how to carry out that which He has given you to do. It is true, there is only one you and only you can run your race!

From Mike's 2010 teaching in Tipp City, OH on CD at CFFM.org, Mike's comments about their life and ministering

It does something when you walk on the grounds here at CFFM; there is peace. Now I know they haven't asked me up here for about 12 years, so maybe I should have a disclaimer up here, "Not necessarily the views of the management". Don't get offended (about something said), if you dislike it, throw it out, just don't get offended! Is that all the further we've come in our life? Now that is scary, Oh Holy Hannah! If that's all the further we've come. Us old people, we've got something to tell, something to tell the youth before they get here! (to old age).

Psalms 132:9 says, *"Let their saints shout for joy."* So raising holy hands, praising; all of this, Jesus Christ is within us, his eyes behind our eyes, his hands behind our hands... Everywhere we walk, we make the imprint of Christ. We need to get radical *inside* of the church!

People ask us how we got started, well, we went to where things were happening, watched and learned, read books, but primarily, got excited about what we were seeing and started trying it out, long before there were prophecies or ordinations over us.

If you only go where you are sitting now and nothing is happening in your life or in the seat next to you, then go to where things are happening! ***The more you allow God to work in the ways He can work, the more He will work!***

Judi: As we walk and we do what we think God is telling us to do at that moment, there may be a prophecy for you and God will tell you. When you are on track, what we all want to do, is serve. When you are doing what God wants you do do, there is no higher calling than to do the will of the Lord and you are doing something, for the next generation.

> ***Matthew** 7:* ***7 & 8***
> *Ask, and it shall be given you; seek, and ye shall find; knock, and it shall be opened unto you*
> *For every one that asketh receiveth; and he that seeketh findeth; and to him that knocketh it shall be opened.*

We hear an expression in Christian culture, *The Lord may use me,* or, *I want the Lord to use me to do His work.* The Lord will not overstep your free will and it has nothing to do with you being worthy or overcoming your own past to do something for God in the future. Remember Paul and King Agrippa in Acts 26? Paul openly lays out all of his own faults and shortcomings but also confesses it is Jesus who gave him the ministry he had after that. God has commissioned us all and given us all the same measure of faith; the faith of Jesus Christ, to carry out that which he has told us to do. We need only to step up and start the work.

Miracle at Youth Camp, Tipp City OH

Mike: At the annual youth camp at our church about four years ago, we had approximately 100 young people who came from all over the country for the teaching of God's Word, to eat, play games and do activities. We are known as Grandma Judi and Grandpa Mike. Our main job is to watch over the kids, pray for them and then we teach them about healing.

After a few days at camp, a young man new to camp and not of our church, Sean Ford, asked if we would pray for him to receive healing in his back that had been injured when a jack slipped beneath a car and he tried to catch it. He had several herniated discs. Prior to this accident, he had been quite a good athlete in basketball and football but he had to give up these sports.

We took him to a quiet corner in the church basement and "spoke to the mountain." We spoke directly to the discs; commanded them to be restored as God had designed them originally. We also spoke directly to the pain.

Immediately he was completely healed! He ran up the basement steps, out into the lawn and was doing calisthenics and all kinds of gyrations. We could have said that he was leaping, jumping and praising Jesus. He began to cry and other campers asked him what was wrong, but these were tears of joy. He said that God immediately healed him in the name of Jesus!

Since this was the early part of August, Sean had already missed quite a bit of weightlifting and other types of activities to prepare for football and, his spot on the football team had been taken by another teammate. However, Sean told his story and the other athlete conceded that Sean was better and gave the spot on the team back to Sean!

We tell people to say three words: "THANK YOU JESUS!" and Sean did share his testimony not only at camp but at other churches. Members of our church got together to see his football and basketball games. He really was a star, all because of Jesus, who is the bright and morning Star. Hallelujah!

•

Judi: We never would have imagined doing all the things we have now done. Healing is a tremendous evangelistic tool and as we know, healing works for people all over the world who have never heard of Jesus or may not even believe in him, but they believe they can be healed.

2015 Israel Pilgrimage

In April of 2015, Pastor Billy Burke of the Miracle Center, Tampa, Florida prophesied over Judi and myself saying we would be taking a trip to Israel in the near future. We really didn't think too much more about it until a pamphlet came in the mail advertising that November 23 – Dec 2, 2015 there was a trip, and, it just seemed like the thing to do, so we signed up.

This trip was really a life-changing experience for us. We saw the mount of Beatitudes, Caesarea Maritima, Nazareth, and Dan Caesarea Philippi by the Jordan River where Judi and I were water-baptized. We went to the Sea of Galilee, Capernaum, the Dead Sea, Jerusalem, the Mount of Olives, Gethsemane, Bethlehem, Mount Zion, the pool of Bethesda, Gordon's Calvary, the garden tomb, and much more.

Even though all of these were impressive, the most exciting thing that we experienced was being able to minister healing to so many people. Dr. Jesus was really doing His thing! We ministered to many people on our bus who were Christians, but also, we ministered to Jews, Muslims and Arabs. As far as we could tell, everyone that we ministered to, were healed.

Generally, I minister in partnership with my wife, Judi, but that night, I was ministering with Ruth Wall, Tonia's mother, who wanted to learn more about ministering. Three ladies came to be healed. At all these healings, their legs were grown out.

I usually say "This is the King's chair, sit down, and Dr. Jesus will work on you!" The person sits down, I gently raise their legs to a comfortable parallel position. You can tell immediately if the legs are uneven. Then by holding the ankles slightly apart, I place my thumbs facing each other on the ankles and, command in the name of Jesus, the legs to even out or to grow out. Many people with back issues can be healed in this way or, in combination with having the person stand, and a command is given for the ligaments, muscles, nerves and tendons of the back to become straightened and strengthened, as well as for the hips to become in alignment.

It just so-happened that all three of these women had one leg shorter than the other. This "growing out the legs" is something that we learned from Charles and Frances Hunter. This technique is handy in healing backs in particular. This is also helpful in increasing the believing or faith of the person that you are going to be ministering to. They can feel it and see with their own eyes that something is going on. Being able to say what part changed or got healed is not really important, it is the fact that they are healed and that someone spoke it into reality.

As people were healed, we started drawing a crowd. One woman comes to mind that had a deformed back and one hip was probably six inches higher than the other. As we ministered to her, I laid my hands on her hips and they began to move. People around us gasped as the power of God went to work. She was so blessed because she did not have any more pain and was able to walk much better.

Encourage people that their complete healing may occur over time. Again, we stress that prayer and ministering are *God Shots* to get the process started.

At any time you sense the person is uncomfortable about being touched, ask their permission. If the recipient is the opposite gender than you, but the same as your partner, have your partner do the laying on of hands. You can also have the recipient put their own hands on the affected area and you can lay your hands on top of theirs. The exception to that are 'private parts' of either gender. We recommend just your hand to their shoulder or hand to hand as you command or pray about those areas.

The ministering of the woman who had had the deformed back was in a hotel where we stayed and took place in view of a shop located in the hotel. An employee was watching what was going on came out so we asked her what she needed. She had two bad knees and arthritis. We told her that was easy, at least for God! Is anything too hard for God? Absolutely not! Well, we ministered to her and her knees were instantly healed and the pain of the arthritis left her.

As we continued to minister to people, more people showed up. Matter of fact, the shop lady's husband said that he wanted what his wife got, so we ministered to him for his bad knees and his arthritis and immediately, he was healed. Hallelujah! As the news spread of these healings, more people wanted to be ministered to the next day. We even had some Jews and Muslims that came. My wife, Judi, is one of the most powerful ladies that I know. She has such great compassion and love for people and she also walks by the spirit and receives revelation a lot easier than I do.

Back to the Jews and the Muslims; we told them that we would minister to them in the name of Jesus. It was amazing to me that they said they believed Jesus could heal them though I'm sure that they did not believe that Jesus is the son of God. Nevertheless, God is so good and his love is so big and powerful, that these men were healed in the name of Jesus.

There was an Arab, Muslim man that approached us for healing and again, he said he believed that

Jesus could heal him. His biggest problem was severely herniated disc in the back. Dr. Jesus took care of that back pain. The pain was gone. God is so good!

•

If you want to see more *God-Shots* opportunities in your life, start doing things you have never done before and then start looking for changes. Try using a different version of your Bible, in conjunction with your favorite always-used one. Stop into a few churches other than the ones in your city. Listen to some teachings from somebody else. Purposely put yourself in places where you are uncomfortable, without the attitude of: *These guys are really messed up; I could teach them a thing or two!* Be humble and thank God for showing you something you didn't know or have not ever experienced. Before long, you will not only see opportunities for others, but, for yourself, also.

Eat the fish, spit out the bones. If flag waving in church is not your thing, just listen to the message, find out why you need to be there. Go and listen to speakers with special gift ministries operating, or get them on CD or DVD.

Dr. Roberts Liardon, Reverend Angus Buchan, Prophet Ben Smith, Pastors Billy Burke, Perry Stone, Joan Hunter, Kenneth Copeland, Joyce Meyer, Creflo Dollar, Joseph Prince and healing evangelist Emily Dotson, to name a few, are known world-wide but there are likely plenty right in your own back yard to choose from. You will also see what God is working across the body of Christ giving you the bigger picture than the church you are most comfortable with and even known by.

Stop in that *Cowboy Up Ministry,* or that motorcycle group church that doubles as a bar at night and a church on Sunday; *Salvation Saloon.* If you are willing to see what you can learn from them, you will see more of God working with you. ***Eat the fish, spit out the bones. Sometimes, what you thought were bones; no good, in the past, are no longer bones!*** *"Life begins at the end of your comfort zone"* is a magnet on our refrigerator that we look at daily.

What about angels and ministering?

Mike: We may do another book and talk about all of that but think about this, if one-third of all the angels were cast down with Satan then two-thirds are still on our side doing something. There are over 300 records in the Word of angels and they are not just showing up before the day of Pentecost. We are reminded in Hebrews:

> ***Hebrews 12:22***
> *But ye are come unto Mount Sion and unto the city of the living God, the heavenly Jerusalem, and to an innumerable company of angels.*

> ***Hebrews 13:2***
> *Be not forgetful to entertain strangers: for thereby some have entertained angels unawares.*

There are different roles and responsibilities for different kinds of angels and with so many references to them, we would be foolish to disregard what we admittedly, do not know a lot about yet.

How do you know when to pray?

Mike: First of all we go to God in the name of Jesus; we call this First Aid. Then, if you are not getting results, then go to another believer to minister to you and believe with you, and if you still have no results, go to the elders in the church, as seen in James 5:14. Don't by-pass your elders. That instruction is in there for a reason but as we say, *God-Shots* can be over time. Finally, if nothing seems to be working, find the best doctor you can and don't condemn yourself.

There are some other things we will touch on that will help (such as forgiveness) in another chapter, but just remember that God gives us everything that pertains to life and Godliness in His Word, or, by direct revelation to us so that we are fully-equipped to handle any situation.

> ***II Timothy 3:16 Amplified version***
> *Every scripture is God-breathed (given by His inspiration) and profitable for instruction, for reproof and conviction of sin, for correction of error and discipline in obedience, (and) for training in righteousness (in holy living, in conformity to God's will in thought, purpose, and action) So that the man of God may be complete and proficient, well-fitted and thoroughly equipped for every good work.*

10 Healing And Miracles

In Hosea 4:6A, God tells us why His people are destroyed: "*My people are destroyed for lack of knowledge*" and it is not a lack of knowledge of the world. As we mentioned earlier, it is because we lack a knowledge of the truth of God's Word, or fail to believe it is the truth; we don't believe the integrity of the Word.

In the Amplified version, I John 3:8 tells us, "*The reason the son of God was made manifest* (visible) *was to undo (destroy, loosen and dissolve) the works the devil (has done).*" This establishes John 10:10 that there are two distinct forces at work in the world, one that works for good, and one that works for evil. We choose who we are going to believe and activate results by what we say, ourselves. People, we are in a spiritual war and what we speak brings tremendous positive or negative outcomes to our lives and that of others.

> ***Proverbs 18:20 & 21***
> *A man's belly shall be satisfied with the fruit of his mouth; and with the increase of his lips shall he be filled. Death and life are in the power of the tongue: and they that love it shall eat the fruit thereof.*

This very thing is the reason some people "lose" their healing. They either do not believe healing is possible, or, they talk themselves out of it afterwards.

There are certain denominations that do not believe that healing is available in this time and day. They believe that healing went out or stopped with the apostles. This truly is a disservice to God the Father, Jesus and their Word. With that attitude and belief, you can see why people have a problem. They have preconceived ideas that negate God's Word. When Jesus was instructing his disciples on how to pray, he stated, that *"Thy* (God's) *kingdom come, Thy will be done in* (on) *earth as it is in heaven."* ***(Matthew 6:9)***.

Let me ask you this: Do you think there is any sickness in heaven? Absolutely not! God wants to have that perfect health on earth, the same as it is in heaven.

Losing The Healing

When people do not have a good foundation of God's Word and have not been instructed that healing is available, many times, it does not stay with them. Some people receive the healing for a day, week, month or even a year but the infirmity comes back. They may get a pain (a lying sign) and they say to themselves "It didn't work", or, "It's back". That is all the devil needs to lay it back on you and he loves it! After all, his *modus operandi,* his *only* goal, in direct opposition to Christ, is this:

> ***John 10:10 Amplified Version***
> *The thief comes* ***only*** *in order to steal and kill and destroy. I came that they may have and enjoy life, and have it in abundance (to the full, till it overflows).*

To give you an example, back about eight years ago, we were having a healing seminar at our house with about 40 participants. We were not ministering that day, Reverend John Shroyer and Reverend Sangat Bains, from India, were running the meeting. Judi's Mother, Margie, had poor hearing in both ears, and one in particular, she calls her "bad ear". The Reverend Bains asked Judi's mother to remove her hearing aids. The two men then ministered to Margie's bad ear and it was immediately healed. She was instructed not to put her hearing aids back in. She told Judi that her bad ear was healed. Judi asked "Well, what about your other ear?" Margie asked for the other ear to be healed, and it was. Glory Hallelujah! God is so good! Praise you, Jesus!

Well, about 5 months later, Margie had some wax build-up and decided to put her hearing aids in and *bingo*, she lost her hearing again which had originally been restored. She thought she was losing the healing but it was only a waxy build-up. She disobeyed the instruction of not putting her hearing aids back in and her hearing was gone. It is so important to do what God says when one is speaking for Him. Listening and obeying are big keys to keeping your healing.

•

Another example is from a visit Judi and I made while ministering healing at Apostle Keith Miller's church in Bradenton, Florida. A woman came up to us with carpel tunnel syndrome. Her left wrist was so bad, she could not pick up and hold her baby. The pain was excruciating. We spoke to the carpel tunnel itself (Matthew 17:20) and the pain and commanded them to come out of her wrist, in the name of Jesus and, it immediately left.

We asked her to thank Jesus and as she was walking away, Judi was inspired to say to her that the pain could come back. The devil likes to come back and test your faith with a false sign but if she would rebuke the pain immediately in the name of Jesus, tell the devil; he is a liar, and she would keep the healing.

We found out that while she was in the shower later that evening that a sharp pain did come back. Now she had a choice to make; she could say the healing must not have worked and taken back the pain, or, do as Judi instructed her to do. The woman chose to tell the devil he was a liar and she was not going there. She said she was healed by the stripes that Jesus bore for her (I Peter 2:24).

Immediately, the pain ceased and never came back. Hallelujah! What a difference the Word of God makes!

God can always do more than what you asked for.

Let's say a person tells you, "I have this pain in my left leg" so you do what you hear God tell to do but does that mean God is going to leave out what you don't know about? You may know something additional has occurred; you see or hear something else after God fixes it right then, or, you and the person you are ministering to may not even know it. God just does what He does and everything gets done.

Remember that "saved" in Romans 10: 9, *(thou shalt be saved)* is the whole package. When we are born-again we should be receiving the whole ball of wax, right there. Physical, mental and spiritual wholeness! We have been short-changing ourselves saying "Well, we have the new birth" and that's enough. No! We should be expecting and receiving physical, mental and spiritual wholeness as well. Let me ask you something else. Do you think this wholeness only applies at the time of the new birth, or, might we be needing that wholeness on an on-going basis? Jesus came to what?

See Isaiah 61: 1 & 2, the prophecy of the purpose of Jesus Christ, and then Jesus reading that prophecy about himself in Luke.

> ***Luke 4:17-19 Amplified Version***
> *17 And there was handed to Him (the roll of) the book of the prophet Isaiah. He unrolled the book and found the place where it was written,*
> *18 The spirit of the Lord is upon Me, because he has anointed Me (the Anointed One, the Messiah) to preach the good news (the Gospel) to the poor; He has sent Me to announce release to the captives and recovery of sight to the blind, to send forth as delivered those who are oppressed (who are downtrodden, bruised, crushed, and broken down by calamity),*
> *19 To proclaim the accepted and acceptable year of the Lord (the day when salvation and the free favors of God profusely abound).*

Salvation is not all that we need. God sends his compassion, it doesn't fail, it is new every morning. Since they are available every day, we must need them, folks. If you have to ask every day or, ten times a day, God is not going to run out, or, withhold His blessings, mercy and compassion!

> ***Lamentations 3:22, 23 Amplified Version***
> *It is because of the Lord's mercy and loving-kindness that we are not consumed, because His (tender) compassions fail not. They are new every morning; great and abundant is Your stability and faithfulness.*

When we are not reigning in life by Christ in a particular area of our life (Romans 5:17), we are cheating ourselves if we don't ask God for help! Sometimes, we think that Jesus is our Savior but after that, he must be sitting on the right hand of God like Lincoln at his marble memorial chair in Washington, D.C.; doing nothing! No! Jesus was a man, but ***is still living now***. He is our intercessor, for one thing, and our advocate, so when you need some intervention, pray to God and thank your brother, Jesus, for getting on the situation.

Hebrews 7:25
Wherefore he (Jesus) *is able to save them to the uttermost that come unto God by him, seeing he ever liveth to make intercession for them.*

Mike: One of my favorite verses is the Amplified Version of Hebrews 2:18.

Hebrews 2:18
For because He Himself (in His humanity) has suffered in being tempted (tested and tried), He is able (immediately) to run to the cry of (assist relieve) those who are being tempted and tested and tried (and who therefore are being exposed to suffering).

We are told in James 4:2 that we have not, because why? We ask not, or, in verse 3; we ask amiss. We also do not dishonor the Father God by offering praise to his son, Jesus. In fact, we are told to do so by Jesus Himself in the Gospel of John.

John 5:23
That all men should honour the Son, even as they honour the Father. He that

honoureth not the Son honoureth not the Father which hath sent him.

We shouldn't be arguing about who to praise; we ought to just be doing it!

The point to remember is that whether we get the miracle of the healing instantaneously is to know that healing is always available to us. We can be healed several times for the same symptoms, or for several different things, as we are told in I Corinthians and that is why God lists it as ***gifts***, plural, for each time is a gift (I Corinthians 12:9). Judi and I have healed people with back problems so many times, we almost never miss it being right away. We were down in an African-American church in Bradenton, FL and the minister, Apostle Keith Miller, let us teach and announced we were going to be doing some healing. 20 came; 15 had bad backs, 15 we grew out the legs and they were all healed, we prayed for one more lady and two people who had arthritis and all 20 received something, they felt the heat and healing of God.

Pastor Billy Burke; the one that prophesied that we would have a ministry in parking lots, grocery stores and airports, is amazing to watch. He was healed as a child at about age 9 by the woman evangelist, Katherine Kuhlman, which is a story in itself *(The Billy Burke Story, www.billyburke.org* Tampa, FL).

After teaching the Word, Billy will call people out of the audience to come forward and then asks them why they came. They may say "Because of the pain" and he will ask them where the pain is. When they go to show him, they realize the pain is already gone; they have been healed on the way down the aisle. That was their move toward receiving. The anointing of healing miracles is so strong on Billy; we just love him! He has had such a good impact on our lives.

Ed note: I was with Mike and Judi at a Pastor Burke teaching and healing service, 2/5/2016 and saw this myself. DVDs available from Christian Retreat.org. (Sarasota, FL)

•

Dr. Roberts Liardon, is not only a great spiritual historian who has spent thousands of hours researching, cataloging and making CDs about the mid-20th-Century healers and evangelists in the world *(God's Generals),* but also has a very dynamic personal history and testimony himself about his walk with Jesus and miracles he has seen and participated in, himself. He was raised up spiritually by his mother and grandmother in a very devoted Christian family.

He has taught in over 120 countries, authored over 60 books. He and his mother, Carol, and staff have been such an inspiration to us. His books are just filled with accounts of super-natural people and experiences. We suggest you go to www.Robertsliardon.org and check out some of his materials. Our point is that God can and does go beyond what we know or even think could happen if we will stop saying "Oh, God would never do that" or "will not work that way".

Created parts or creative miracles fall into this category... It is hard to believe it is even possible, but why wouldn't God be able to install a new part if one is needed? Some people are born congenitally with missing limbs or body parts, or, their parts are worn out or damaged or amputated.

> ***Genesis 18:14a Amplified***
> *Is anything too hard or too wonderful for*

the Lord?

We know from the Word there are different types of healings; cures, restoration and, *wholeness* is everything that pertains to us; body, soul and spirit, so let us not limit God by thinking a replacement part cannot be installed. You can read more about this by doing an Internet search on any healer and the testimonies that are listed.

Obstacles to Healing

These may not only be regarding the person's belief of the Word but may involve other people. You may have heard of the phrase *Paul's thorn in the flesh* for which, some great people think he had an affliction, but it was the people around him that satan sent to buffet; torment, Paul. (II Corinthians 12: 7). Even Jesus had to deal with peoples' unbelief. When he was ministering in his home town, Nazareth, he could not do much there because of their unbelief (Matthew 13:58, Luke 4:24) and in another instance, when ministering Jesus had to take the man out of town to remove him from the negative believing influence of the community (Mark 8:22-23).

Since God wants us to "*prosper and be in health*" above all things (III John 2), knowing this, then we have to see if there are nay-sayers or negative people about that are influencing the outcome. If so, you can just have everyone else leave, or you leave with the person to a private place to do the ministering. (Mark 5:35-42)

Faith of a mustard seed. How much "faith" is enough?

As you might know, that grain of a mustard seed that is planted and the ratio of the plant that it grows into is very different. It just means, it takes what it takes to get the job done and you can't determine where people are in their "believing" or that the person said they are not sure they can believe God will do it, but He does do it and they are healed anyway.

Sometimes our believing overrides what the person feels or says; some people call this *getting on my faith,* so the person gets healed, regardless of where their education is or what their verbalization about the situation is. There is no magic formula to "how much is enough?" There are also records of parents' believing for the child and the one to be healed is not even present. Why, sometimes, even dead for hours and they got healed because of the actions of the parent! (II Kings 4: 1-36)

We have seen healing take place by a group being ministered to at one time, or, something is called out to the audience.

We were in South Carolina with a group once and the teaching minister called out "metal in the body" to the audience. Another minister was sitting beside us who had a plate and screws in his ankle and had never been able to rotate his ankle for 23 years; like it was frozen and could not be rotated. He stood up and the immobility and the metal were gone and he was able to rotate it! He shook his head and laughed and declared that "was unbelievable!" that he could now rotate his foot, but, he did and no one touched him at all.

Giving up medication or support aids

In ministering, we do not tell people to stop taking medicines or throw away their canes, braces or supports. They decide how they want to handle that in their own life and if they go to their physician to confirm the healing or not. We DO ask them to do something they could not do before and then to start praising and thanking Jesus and the Father for their healing. We do want them to acknowledge that something has happened, and again, they may not have full healing right then, though they may feel heat or movement of some kind and the rest happens over time and the pain is gone.

Building up yourselves in the Word

We want to remember to spend more and more time in the Word, building ourselves up so we are prepared. We are like an athlete, we have that endurance and spiritual fortitude when we are called on; for ourselves or for others, when it is needed.

> ***Romans 10:17***
> *So then, faith cometh by hearing, and hearing by the word of God.*

We need to spend time in the Word of God. Get into a spirit-filled church where the Word is taught with accuracy and where the Holy Spirit is being manifested. Surround yourself with other believers that are excited about Jesus and have a positive mind-set; not a bunch of whiners or criticizers. Make a mental picture of what you need and keep it in mind often, praying for it until it comes into manifestation. Have patience, for what God has promised in His Word, He is more than willing to perform, in your lives.

Mike: Sometimes, there is so much present with a person, but we just go boldly before the throne and expect help (Hebrews 4:16). We trust in God and Dr. Jesus, always, to do the job. It's not our power.

Mike: The first few times **I felt the pain of the other person,** I thought something was wrong with me! After awhile, I learned that it was God working with me to identify things with that person.

Not long ago, I woke up with a pain in my right knee, which means, many times, that I will run into a person that has a problem with a knee. God gives me pains some times as a form of Word of Knowledge. Judi and I went out for an early morning breakfast and I continued to get that knee pain. We had a friend with us at breakfast and I told him and Judi that there must be someone in the restaurant that had a bad knee but no one we spoke with had a knee problem.

For the rest of the day, I continued to have that pain. Once it became evening, I thought that maybe I had misunderstood and it really was me with the problem! We were at home and about 7:30 P.M., there was a knock on the door and it was a gentleman friend of ours who wanted to have prayer for a situation, so we prayed with him and then he told us about his son who is living with him.

The son was injured in the military and he had so much pain that he could not stand up long for very long and it was difficult to climb stairs. We suggested we go to the man's home and when we arrived, the father introduced us and I told the son that we pray for people and that in many cases, people receive healing right away.

The first thing that I noticed was that the son had a knee support on the right knee. Wow! This has to be the person God wants healed; it was the right knee after all! I mentioned that my knee had shown pain and that God wanted him healed. He said he had been looking for his knee brace and had just found it that morning. God is so cool!

We told him a few testimonies that would build his believing in God and then we ministered to his knee. We commanded the knee to be healed in the name of Jesus and also for the pain to leave. We said “Now move it, how does it feel?” He could move it without any pain. Hallelujah! God is good and Dr. Jesus comes through again! We also took trauma and stress off him in the name of Jesus.

Next, we had him sit in a chair to see if one leg was longer than the other. Sure enough, one was over an inch longer so we told him to keep his eyes open and see what God would do. We asked his girlfriend and the father to come close so they could see it, too. We prayed and commanded the leg to grow and become the same length as the other and immediately, it did grow out. He felt it move and became excited.

Now we were ready for that damaged and frozen back. He could not bend over more than a few degrees but once we took authority over his back and the sciatic nerve, we commanded it to be restored and the pain to leave. We asked him to bend over and touch his toes and to move his hips around and then we asked him how he felt. He first started laughing and then it turned into tears of joy and rejoicing. He was healed, no pain and set free of the devil's hold. Glory to God the Father and thank you Jesus! God is good all the time. Naturally, my pain was also gone, thanks be to God.

When you minister, you keep working with the individual until all things are taken care of and God will tell you things to speak or what to do. Have people thank Jesus right away. We asked them to say three words, "Thank you Jesus! Then we have them do something they have not been able to do before the healing. Encourage them to fortify themselves in God's Word and to share their story about their healing and for them to heal others, too. These are the keys to keeping the healing.

11 Mixing In Faith

Well, what is Faith?

Hebrews 11:1
Now faith is the substance of things hoped for, the evidence of things not seen.

Hebrews 11:1 ***Amplified Version***
Now faith is the assurance (the confirmation, the title deed) of the things (we) hope for, being the proof of things (we) do not see and the conviction of their reality (faith perceiving as real fact what is not revealed to the senses).

Faith is the title deed to everything that is

promised in the Word of God. Faith is having confidence in something that has already been done over 2000 years ago. Faith is believing the finished work that Jesus accomplished through His perfect walk with the Father, His punishment for our sins, His death, His Resurrection, and His outpouring of the Holy Spirit.

> **Philippians 4:13**
> *I can do all things through Christ which strengtheneth me.*

> **Philippians 4:13** ***Amplified Version***
> *I have strength for all things in Christ Who empowers me (I am ready for anything and equal to anything through Him Who infuses inner strength into me; I am self-sufficient in Christ's sufficiency.*

We have to get this deep down into the most inner part of our mind. The biggest battle is between our ears. We need to tame our mind; renew it to the Word of God. If we fortify the Word in our mind it will prevent the devil from taking from us what God has already given us.

The Manifestation of Faith

Most Christian groups would call this "the gift" of Faith. We do not have a problem with this and don't think it is necessary to have division over it and here is a tip that we have learned along the way: if you disagree with something someone says or does, just keep working to keep unity in the Body of Christ.

Back to **I Corinthians 12:1** *"Now concerning spiritual gifts, brethren, I would not have you ignorant,"* the word "gifts" is in italics in King James. This indicates that it is not in the Greek texts; the translators added it. The word "spiritual" is the Greek word *pneumatikos.* A better translation would be "spiritual matters" or "things".

If you want to use the word "gifts", go ahead. The only thing we are concerned about is that people will say that a person has the gift of healing, the gift of prophecy and so on, when every born-again believer has the ability to do all nine manifestations.

A key component here is that God doesn't want you to be ignorant about these things, He wants you *to know to the point of being able to use, and receive and grow in knowledge.*

Verse 7 of I Corinthians 12 states: "*But the manifestation of the Spirit is given to every man to profit withal.*" He has given them to us. If they truly are ours, then He wants us to know as much as possible about them.

Verse 8 begins telling us the different benefits or profits given to every man. The "one" in verse 8 refers back to "profit" in verse 7.

> ***I Corinthians 12:8-10***
> *8 For to one* (profit or benefit) *is given by the Spirit the word of wisdom; to another* (for another profit) *word of knowledge by the same Spirit;*
> *9 to another the faith by the same Spirit; to another the gifts of healing by the same Spirit,*
> *10 To another the working of miracles; to another prophecy; to another discerning of spirits; to another divers kinds of tongues; to another the interpretation of tongues.*

Verse 11 then clearly states, "*but all these worketh that one and the selfsame Spirit dividing to every man severally as he will."* **He** is a pronoun that, by the rules of grammar, refer back to its closest noun, **man**. (This fits with verse 7 – He has given it to every man…)

Now we know, as a believer, we all have the measure of faith *(Romans 12:3)* but this listing of *faith* goes beyond "the measure", otherwise, why would it be listed as a manifestation? Let us give you a few definitions of the manifestation of faith that we have come across:

The manifestation of faith is to manifest the ability which God gives of absolute faith and confidence to do whatever God tells you.

(This is very close to the former)
The manifestation of faith is to exercise the authority and ability, which God gives, of absolute trust and confidence to do whatever God tells you.

At times when the gift or manifestation of faith is being operated, a minister has the ability to bring about signs, miracles and wonders as the Holy Spirit leads.

For years, Judi and I have been ministering healing to peoples' backs. It is almost a 100% done-deal when we minister to them they will be healed. Why? Because of the faith that we have. We have seen it hundreds of times. We have no doubt; absolute confidence, that God will heal them. Hallelujah!! Praise the Lord!

I tell you one thing, we have to take it to the streets, we've got to take it to the streets! Do you hear me? We have to take it to the streets! I keep saying it, but we can't just be in these four walls of the church and I know many of us are venturing outside the church.

This thing with my Ordination, Praise the Lord, I wrestled with it, I thank God for it, for it has opened so many doors. Of course people are out there clapping when you are ordained; they clap for you...wonderful, wonderful... But regardless of their applause or not, I have to have sold-out commitment.

See that's the thing, God will give it to you but you have to be willing to go out there and do something. Actually, it's the other way around. You just start in doing and God will be showing up. We all have the same ability, just some use it, some don't; or, only use it certain places and times where it *seems* God would be at work. We just need to take Him at His Word and do what He says... Many, many things we have seen happen, that, in former times, we would have said *God won't*, or *God can't* do something a particular way, but when we got to the point where we said *Let 'er rip, God*, **then** we started seeing the miraculous!

How do we get faith?

Romans 10:17 instructs, "*So then, faith cometh by hearing, and hearing by the word of God.*" We need to spend time in the Word of God. Get into a spirit-filled church where the Word is taught with accuracy and where the Holy Spirit is being manifested. Surround yourself with other believers that are excited about Jesus and have a positive mind-set; not a bunch of whiners.

Make a mental picture of what you need and want to do for God, keep it in mind often, praying for it until it comes into manifestation. Have patience, for what God has promised in His Word, He is more than willing to perform, in your lives.

12 The Devil Doesn't Heal

A few years ago when Judi and I were on a cruise in the middle of the Atlantic Ocean, God gave me a revelation that He is the only healer. It was so exciting that as God was giving me the revelation, I spoke it to Judi and I also said "There is more"!

One of the questions that I always wondered about, is how a witch doctor could do all of his gyrations over a person and they would be healed? God followed up with the revelation that it was God's "immutable law of believing". The believing of the witch doctor and the sick person and any other people involved, brought about the healing. That revelation settled it for me.

Believing works for saints and sinners alike.

People can choose whatever they like but for me, I am convinced that the devil does not heal and anything that he does as far as imitating the manifestations of Holy Spirit, are completely counterfeit. We talked about the opposite natures of Christ and the devil in John 10:10 and we can determine the responsibilities of the devil (lucifer, the fallen angel) and that of our Lord and Savior Jesus Christ.

> ***I Peter 5:8***
> *Be sober, be vigilant; because your adversary the devil, as a roaring lion, walketh about, seeking whom he may devour.*

Let's face it, the devil is bad and God is good, always. Besides saying that the devil heals, some say that God makes people sick to test, or try, or to humble them. Many God-fearing wonderful believers have things flip-flopped. One of the things that we need to remember is that sickness comes from the devil and a good portion of the time, is caused by devil spirits.

Once the spirit has been removed, the healing can take place. In chapter three of Mark, after Jesus had been healing and casting out spirits, they accused Jesus of having Beelzebub, and by the prince of devils, he was casting out devils. In verse 23b of that same chapter, Jesus asks his disciples "How can satan cast out satan?"

> ***Mark 3:24-26***
> *24 And if a kingdom be divided against itself, that kingdom cannot stand.*
> *25 And if a house be divided against itself, that house cannot stand.*
> *26 And if satan rise up against himself, and can be divided, he cannot stand, but hath an end.*

Thus, if satan would cast out devils and also heal, his kingdom would be open to destruction by the same logic. We know that in Mark 13:22 we are told:

> ***Mark 13:22***
> *For false Christs and false prophets shall rise, and shall shew signs and wonders, to seduce, if it were possible, even the elect.*

These "false prophets" are not surprising because we read about Moses and Arron when they approached the Pharaoh, that the magicians' staffs became snakes, manifested by the power of the devil. However, Moses' staff also became a snake and devoured the snakes that the devil brought into manifestation!

Even though the devil can produce signs and wonders, nowhere in the Word does it say he ever healed someone. Anything he does in regard to the things of God's nine manifestations, ***are all counterfeit.***

Some people have seen videos of psychic healings taking place in the Philippines. The person performing this feat would use his finger to open up the torso of a person and then supernaturally, seal up the wound. This does not mean they were healed.

Even with today's medical procedures, when a person has an operation for cancer, the doctor makes an incision and removes the tumor. That still doesn't mean that they are healed. In almost all cases, the doctors recommend chemotherapy or radiation because they believe, for the most part, the person is not completely healed with surgery alone. Only God can do the healing, either supernaturally or, naturally, as God designed the body to heal itself.

God's Word prophesied that a Messiah would come to save his people and one of the signs they would know that this person was ***the*** Christ, ***the*** anointed one, is that he would heal a man that was born blind.

> ***John 9:32 & 33***
> *Since the world began, was it not heard that any man opened the eyes of one that was born blind. If this man were not of God, he could do nothing".*

If the adversary was able to heal, he would have taken advantage of this prophecy before Christ arrived on the scene and would have said he was the true son of God!

In ***John chapter 10***, shortly after Jesus Christ declared, "*the thief cometh not but for to steal, and to kill and to destroy,"* he says in *verses 19-21:*

> ***John 10:19-21***
> *19 There was a division therefore again among the Jews for these sayings.*
> *20 And many of them said "He hath a devil, and is mad; why hear ye him?*

> *21 Others said, These are not the words of him that hath a devil. Can a devil open the eyes of the blind?*

That says it all!! I believe this could have easily been a period for the punctuation mark in verse 21, not a question mark.

The answer to that question is, THE DEVIL WAS NOT ABLE TO HEAL and he is unable to heal unto this day. Glory Hallelujah!!!

13 Healing Scriptures

Here is a list of scriptures compiled by Dorothy Kozar, with our thanks, that you can use to get yourself started on knowing more of God's Word in your life. They will help you to get started in keeping them in your mind to pull down strongholds in your own mind (II Corinthians 10:5) or from other peoples' mouths when they say that it is not God's will or even available for them to be healed. We have to get to the point that we are super-naturally driven in our thinking and response; immediately, and not be circumstance conditioned. Just remember that what something looks or sounds like, if it doesn't line up with the Word of God, is irrelevant to God.

Following these, we will wrap it all up with more

on that powerful name of Jesus and His last words of instruction to us while He was still on earth.

Genesis 20:17
So Abraham prayed unto God: and God healed Abimelech, and his and his wife, and his maidservants; and they bare children.

I Chronicles 16:8-12
*8 G*ive thanks unto the Lord, call upon his name, make known his deeds among the people.
9 Sing unto him, sing psalms unto him, talk ye of all his wondrous works.
10 Glory ye in his holy name: let the heart of them rejoice that seek the Lord.
11 Seek the Lord and his strength, seek his face continually.
12 Remember his marvelous works that he hath done, his wonders, and the judgments of his mouth.

II Chronicles 30:20
And the Lord hearkened to Hezekiah, and healed the people.

Psalms 103:1-6

1 Bless the Lord, O my soul: and all that is
within me, bless his holy name.
2 Bless the Lord, O my soul, and forget not
all his benefits:
3 Who forgiveth all thine iniquities; who
healeth all thy diseases;
4 Who redeemeth thy life from destruction;
who crowneth thee with lovingkindness
and tender mercies;
5 Who satisfieth thy mouth with good
things; so that thy youth is renewed like the
eagle's.
6 The Lord executeth righteousness and
judgment for all that are oppressed.

Psalm 107:20

He sent his word, and healed them, and delivered them from their destructions.

Isaiah 53:5

But he was wounded for our transgressions, he was bruised for our iniquities: the chastisement of our peace was upon him; and with his stripes we are healed.

Jeremiah 17:14
Heal me, O Lord, and I shall be healed; save me, and I shall be saved: for thou art my praise.

Psalms 30:2
O Lord my God, I cried unto thee, and thou hast healed me.

Matthew 4:23 & 24
And Jesus went about all Galilee, teaching in their synagogues, and preaching the gospel of the kingdom, and healing all manner of sickness and all manner of disease among the people.
And his fame went throughout all Syria: and they brought unto him all sick people that were taken with divers diseases and torments, and those which were possessed with devils, and those which were lunatick, and those that had the palsy; and he healed them.

Matthew 8:5-8
5 And when Jesus was entered into
Capernaum, there came unto him a

centurion, beseeching him,
6 And saying, Lord, my servant lieth at home sick of the palsy, grievously tormented.
7 And Jesus saith unto him, I will come and heal him.
8 The centurion answered and said, Lord, I am not worthy that thou shouldest come under my roof: but speak the word only, and my servant shall be healed.

Matthew 8:13
And Jesus said unto the centurion, Go thy way; and as thou hast believed, so be it done unto thee. And his servant was healed in the selfsame hour.

Matthew 8:16
When the even was come, they brought unto him many that were possessed with devils: and he cast out the spirits with his word, and healed all that were sick.

Matthew 9:28 & 29
And when he was come into the house, the blind men came to him: and Jesus saith unto them, Believe ye that I am able to do

this? They said unto him, Yea, Lord. Then touched he their eyes, saying, According to your faith be it unto you.

Matthew 9:35

And Jesus went about all the cities and villages, teaching in their synagogues, and preaching the gospel of the kingdom, and healing every sickness and every disease among the people.

Matthew 10:1

And when he had called unto him his twelve disciples, he gave them power against unclean spirits, to cast them out, and to heal all manner of sickness and all manner of disease.

Matthew 10:7 & 8

And as ye go, preach, saying, The kingdom of heaven is at hand. Heal the sick, cleanse the lepers, raise the dead, cast out devils: freely ye have received, freely give.

Matthew 11:5

The blind receive their sight, and the lame walk, the lepers are cleansed, and the deaf hear, the dead are raised up, and the poor have the gospel preached to them.

Matthew 12:15

But when Jesus knew it, he withdrew himself from thence: and great multitudes followed him, and he healed them all.

Mark 1:34

And he healed many that were sick of divers diseases, and cast out many devils; and suffered not the devils to speak, because they knew him.

Mark 3:10

For he had healed many; insomuch that they pressed upon him for to touch him, as many as had plagues.

Mark 5:23

And besought him greatly, saying, My little daughter lieth at the point of death: I pray thee, come and lay thy hands on her, that she may be healed; and she shall live.

Mark 5:29

And straightway the fountain of her blood

was dried up; and she felt in her body that she was healed of that plague.

Mark 6:13

And they cast out many devils, and anointed with oil many that were sick, and healed them.

Mark 9:23

Jesus said unto him, If thou canst believe, all things are possible to him that believeth.

Mark 11:24

Therefore I say unto you, What things soever ye desire, when ye pray, believe that ye receive them, and ye shall have them.

Luke 4:18

The Spirit of the Lord is upon me, because he hath anointed me to preach the gospel to the poor; he hath sent me to heal the brokenhearted, to preach deliverance to the captives, and recovering of sight to the blind, to set at liberty them that are bruised.

Luke 4:40

Now when the sun was setting, all they that

had any sick with divers diseases brought them unto him; and he laid his hands on every one of them, and healed them.

Luke 5:15

But so much the more went there a fame abroad of him: and great multitudes came together to hear, and to be healed by him of their infirmities.

Luke 6:17-19

17 And he came down with them, and
stood in the plain, and the company of his
disciples, and a great multitude of people
out of all Judaea and Jerusalem, and from
the sea coast of Tyre and Sidon, which
came to hear him, and to be healed of their
diseases;
18 And they that were vexed with unclean
spirits: and they were healed.
19 And the whole multitude sought to
touch him: for there went virtue out of him,
and healed them all.

Luke 7:21-23

21 And in that same hour he cured many of
their infirmities and plagues, and of evil

spirits; and unto many that were blind he gave sight.
22 Then Jesus answering said unto them, Go your way, and tell John what things ye have seen and heard; how that the blind see, the lame walk, the lepers are cleansed, the deaf hear, the dead are raised, to the poor the gospel is preached.
23 And blessed is he, whosoever shall not be offended in me.

Luke 8:2

And certain women, which had been healed of evil spirits and infirmities, Mary called Magdalene, out of whom went seven devils.

Luke 8:36

They also which saw it told them by what means he that was possessed of the devils was healed.

Luke 8:47

And when the woman saw that she was not hid, she came trembling, and falling down before him, she declared unto him before all the people for what cause she had touched him, and how she was healed immediately.

Luke 9:6
And they departed, and went through the towns, preaching the gospel, and healing every where.

Luke 9:11
And the people, when they knew it, followed him: and he received them, and spake unto them of the kingdom of God, and healed them that had need of healing.

Luke 9:42
And as he was yet a coming, the devil threw him down, and tare him. And Jesus rebuked the unclean spirit, and healed the child, and delivered him again to his father.

Luke 10:9
And heal the sick that are therein, and say unto them, The kingdom of God is come nigh unto you.

Luke 13:11-13
11 And, behold, there was a woman which

had a spirit of infirmity eighteen years, and
was bowed together, and could in no wise
lift up herself.
12 And when Jesus saw her, he called her
to him, and said unto her, Woman, thou art
loosed from thine infirmity.
13 And he laid his hands on her: and
immediately she was made straight, and
glorified God.

Luke 14:4

And they held their peace. And he took him, and healed him, and let him go.

Luke 17:12-19

12 And as he entered into a certain village,
there met him ten men that were lepers,
which stood afar off:
13 And they lifted up their voices, and said,
Jesus, Master, have mercy on us.
14 And when he saw them, he said unto
them, Go shew yourselves unto the
priests. And it came to pass, that, as they
went, they were cleansed.
15 And one of them, when he saw that he
was healed, turned back, and with a loud
voice glorified God.

16 And fell down on his face at his feet, giving him thanks: and he was a Samaritan.
17 And Jesus answering said, Were there not ten cleansed? but where are the nine?
18 There are not found that returned to give glory to God, save this stranger.
19 And he said unto him, Arise, go thy way: thy faith hath made thee whole.

Luke 22:51

And Jesus answered and said, Suffer ye thus far. And he touched his ear, and healed him.

John 5:13

And he that was healed wist not who it was: for Jesus had conveyed himself away, a multitude being in that place.

John 12:1

Then Jesus six days before the Passover came to Bethany, where Lazarus was which had been dead, whom he raised from the dead.

John 14:12

Verily, verily, I say unto you, He that

believeth on me, the works that I do shall he do also; and greater works than these shall he do; because I go unto my Father.

Acts 3:11

And as the lame man which was healed held Peter and John, all the people ran together unto them in the porch that is called Solomon's, greatly wondering.

Acts 4:14

And beholding the man which was healed standing with them, they could say nothing against it.

Acts 4:22

For the man was above forty years old, on whom this miracle of healing was shewed.

Acts 5:16

There came also a multitude out of the cities round about unto Jerusalem, bringing sick folks, and them which were vexed with unclean spirits: and they were healed every one.

Acts 8:7

For unclean spirits, crying with loud voice, came out of many that were possessed with them: and many taken with palsies, and that were lame, were healed.

Acts 9:36-42
36 Now there was at Joppa a certain
disciple named Tabitha, which by
interpretation is called Dorcas: this woman
was full of good works and almsdeeds
which she did.
37 And it came to pass in those days, that
she was sick, and died: whom when they
had washed, they laid her in an upper
chamber.
38 And forasmuch as Lydda was nigh to
Joppa, and the disciples had heard that
Peter was there, they sent unto him two
men, desiring him that he would not delay
to come to them.
39 Then Peter arose and went with them.
When he was come, they brought him into
the upper chamber: and all the widows
stood by him weeping, and shewing the
coats and garments which Dorcas made,
while she was with them.

> 40 But Peter put them all forth, and kneeled down, and prayed; and turning him to the body said, Tabitha, arise. And she opened her eyes: and when she saw Peter, she sat up.
> 41 And he gave her his hand, and lifted her up, and when he had called the saints and widows, presented her alive.
> 42 And it was known throughout all Joppa; and many believed in the Lord.

Mike:
That healing of the dog? I didn't forget!

Back in 1977 when were were living in Grand Rapids, MI, we went over to Tom and Connie's home just to chat. They had a dog with a cancerous tumor on his back. At just four years old, Alfie couldn't even go up and down the stairs and the vet wanted to euthanize it but Tom and Connie asked if the dog could be healed.

We sat there and visited and in retrospect, I really believe that God was preparing the way for us to minister, heal and deliver people by the dog getting delivered first. We had never prayed about anything like this before but I put my hand on the dog's back and I prayed, and, the lump disappeared.! Before we left, the dog was running up and down the stairs! This was the first time that we prayed for anything and it immediately got healed! We were amazed, and, Alfie lived another ten years.

If God will do that for a dog, what will He do for you? If you are hesitant to try ministering to people, why not start with your pet?

One of the other pet healings was down in North Carolina. "Doodles" was his name and he had been limping for two years since the last time we had visited. When we were about ready to leave and the owners, Sue and Chuck, set the dog on the counter, and we knew that it had a spirit of arthritis which can be taken out right away. Judi and I commanded the arthritis to come out. We told them the dog may limp out of habit, but it did not limp, it just took off, completely healed! Doodles was running all over the yard!

We have suggested to people they minister to their pets, then those people have testimonies of healing, also!

14 That Wonderful And Powerful Name Of Jesus

There is so much power and authority in the name of Jesus, particularly when it comes off the lips of a believer in faith and believing. We need to be fully-persuaded that name is above all other names. It can be spoken as Jesus, Jesus Christ, Christ Jesus or Jesus of Nazareth. The main thing is you get "Jesus" in the command. With all these names, the devil kingdom quakes at the name of Jesus!

Proverbs 22:1
A good name is rather to be chosen than great riches, and loving favour rather than

silver and gold.

Truly, the name that the Father chose for his only begotten son has great riches and loving favor. I think the best name God has given us is that of a son or daughter of God. There is not a better name for one of the Father God's children than son of God.

> ***Matthew 1:21***
> *And she shall bring forth a son, and thou shalt call his name Jesus: for he shall save his people from their sins.*

Jesus means "Jehovah our savior". Joshua in Hebrew in the Old Testament means the same.

Matthew 18:20
For where two or three are gathered together in my name (Jesus), *there am I in the midst of them.*

Mark 16:17
And these signs shall follow them that believe; in my name shall they cast out devils; they shall speak with new tongues.

John 14:13 & 14
And whatsoever ye shall ask in my name, that will I do, that the Father may be glorified in the Son. If ye shall ask any thing in my name, I will do it.

John 20: 31
But these (this book) *are written, that ye might believe that Jesus is the Christ, the Son of God; and that believing ye might have life through his name.*

Acts 4:12
Neither is their salvation in any other: for there is none other name under heaven given among men, whereby we must be saved.

Acts 10:48a
And he commanded them to be baptized in the name of the Lord.

Philippians 2:9
Wherefore God also hath highly exalted him, and given him a name which is above every name .

Father God gave Jesus a name above all names. Why? Because Jesus humbled himself, was obedient even unto death. He gave up his reputation and became a servant. ***Think about this:*** Every name, everything; whether it is cancer, an infirmity, sickness devil spirits, financial problems or poverty, all has to bow and go, in the name of Jesus. Hallelujah!

> ***Philippians 2:10***
> *That at the name of Jesus every knee should bow, of things in heaven, and things in earth, and things under the earth.*

It is important it is to put that name in our tool box to fight the fight against our adversary; the devil and his cohorts. Don't be afraid to use the **name of Jesus**.
People talk about using the Lord's name in vain, thinking it is just in what we would call cursing.

Actually, Judi and I believe *taking the Lord's name in vain* is in using the name of Jesus and not expecting results! When we bless our food, in the name of Jesus, we expect this food becomes supernatural as it enters our body and if there is anything harmful present, that it is removed. The same is true when we commanded cancer or any disease to leave, in the name of Jesus. We like the song *There Is Power In The Name Of Jesus*. It finishes with the words *break every chain.* Hallelujah!

That name does break the chains that bind. People are set free from death, diseases, mental prisons, financial situations and spiritual bondage. Yes—there is power in the name of Jesus!

Thank you, Jesus!

15 Epilogue

What happens next in the story is up to you and the Father, and your journey with Dr. Jesus! If you knew you were going to die and had called all of your family and friends together to have a conversation with them, wouldn't that be weighty? Wouldn't it have some significance to it? Before Jesus ascended into heaven, he made some great instructions and statements for us.

Acts 1:8

But ye shall receive power, after that the Holy Ghost (Spirit) *is come upon you: and ye shall be witnesses unto me both in Jerusalem, and in all Judaea, and in Samaria, and unto the uttermost part of the earth.*

Ye shall receive Power:

That power is the Greek word *dunamis* and it means an inherent (potential) power. We get our English word dynamite from *dunamis.* Can you imagine that? A powerful force contained in your body that can be activated by speaking the Word of God with faith and believing. Remember, we have Christ in us, the Hope of glory.

The second thing in the verse to note is that Jesus was speaking not only to those people at the time this was written, but it still reigns supreme in our day and time; that you are still to be witnesses unto the uttermost part of the earth.

Do you think that includes your town, village or city, your family? Absolutely! Just look around. What do we see in the world today? Do we see needs that need to be met? God has a solution for every problem that the world throws at you!

We suggest that you read the book of Acts and search for the dynamics of the First Century Church. This is the only book in the Bible that does not have an Amen, or an ending.

The book of Acts is continuing, even in our generation today. We can and should be writing a chapter, day by day, week by week and year by year. We want it to continue to live until the day Christ comes back for his church.

Mark 16:15
And he said unto them, Go ye into all the world, and preach the gospel to every creature.

Our prayer is that what we have written in this book will settle these matters in your life or at least, give you some food for thought. If for some reason, you have been taught differently than how we presented things, you research it. It is not meant to offend anyone.

God bless you mightily in the name above all names, Jesus Christ. You use that name in healing and deliverance for the glory of God the Father and His Son, Jesus!

Additional Reading

Suggested reading, though many of these authors have several publications:

1. Christ The Healer, F.F. Bosworth
2. Healing The Whole Man, Joan Hunter
3. How To Heal The Sick, Charles & Frances Hunter
4. Jesus The Healer, E.W. Kenyon
5. The Glory of God, Guillermo Maldonado
6. God's Generals, Dr. Roberts Liardon
7. Freedom From Fatal Thinking, Billy Burke
8. Deliver Us From Evil, Don Basham
9. Angels: Knowing their Purpose, Charles & Annette Capps
10. How To Turn Your Faith Loose, Kenneth E. Hagin
11. The Battlefield Of The Mind, Joyce Meyer
12. Satan's Generals: Overcoming Principalities and Powers, Dr. Madelene Eayrs, Michael Kleu

About the Co-Author: Jeannie Hill, B.S., CHM, CCST has been involved with home fellowships and public churches for many years contributing teachings, music and song. With her writing and editing, she has published in magazines, newspapers and an on-line blog. This is her second book. She can be reached at jean.hill555@gmail.com

36463856R20123

Made in the USA
San Bernardino, CA
24 July 2016